FROM THE FILMS OF

Harry Potter™

— OFFICIAL —
CHRISTMAS
COOKBOOK

FROM THE FILMS OF

Harry Potter

— OFFICIAL —
CHRISTMAS
COOKBOOK

Text by Jody Revenson
Recipes by Elena P. Craig

INSIGHT
EDITIONS

CONTENTS

Chapter Five
DESSERTS

Chapter Six
DRINKS

Chapter Seven
HARRY POTTER HOLIDAY-THEMED PARTIES

INTRODUCTION

— ✳ —

Christmas in the Harry Potter films is filled with garlands of pine and fir, trees and wreaths decorated with shining gold stars, cards strung on ribbons, flickering candles, and ghostly carolers. Traditional English Christmas crackers grace tables everywhere, whether at Number Twelve, Grimmauld Place, where the Weasleys enjoy the holiday with Harry and Hermione in *Harry Potter and the Order of the Phoenix*; at the Weasleys' home, The Burrow, in *Harry Potter and the Half-Blood Prince*; or on the tables in the Great Hall in *Harry Potter and the Sorcerer's Stone*. When Harry stays at Hogwarts School of Witchcraft and Wizardry during his first year, snow not only falls outside the walls of the castle, but also within the Great Hall, where there are Christmas dinners for the students with bright oranges, tasty roasts, and cakes topped with wizard snowmen carrying brooms. It is the gathering of friends and family at Christmas—no matter where and no matter who—and the sharing a hearty meal and sweet confections that enhances the magic of the holiday.

Inspired by the wizarding world, *Harry Potter: Official Christmas Cookbook* offers everything from soup to nuts for holiday celebrations—Nicolas Flamel Vichyssoise Soup (page 34) to Slug Club Christmas Party Spiced Nuts (page 23), of course—as well as hearty entrées, hot and crusty breads, enchanting desserts, and drinks that will raise everyone's spirits. The dishes within this book are inspired by the Harry Potter films, and there are so many even the 100-foot-long tables in the Great Hall might not be able to hold them all. The pumpkin patch on the Hogwarts grounds would be a perfect place to acquire the ingredients for Hagrid's One-Pot Pumpkin Stew (page 36) or Hagrid's Pumpkin Seed Brittle (page 89), and the greenhouses outside the castle might grow the vegetables for Sprout's Superior Sprouts (page 45) or the Greenhouse Greens Salad entrée (page 59).

Molly Weasley inspired a Weasley Sweater Focaccia (page 53), and the Divination class's Tessomancy teacups can be found in Professor Trelawney's Pots de Crème dessert (page 123). There are Yule Ball dishes that echo the seafood served on screen, and a selection of colorful punches that represent the three schools that compete in the Triwizard Tournament. Drinks include a Magical Mulled Wine (page 149), Hot Chocolate Brooms (page 137), and a Mistletoe Cocktail (Nargle-free) (page 150) for getting warmed up during the cold, wintry days.

No meal would be complete without captivating confections, some inspired by the sweets sold at Honeydukes in Hogsmeade such as Every Flavor Cake Pops (page 91). Traditional English desserts—called puddings in Great Britain—are also included, like Professor Flitwick's Christmas Figgy Pudding (page 128), a Triwizard Trifle (page 131), and Harry's Favorite Treacle Tart (page 101).

Each easy-to-follow recipe lists vegan, vegetarian, and gluten-free options with consideration toward everybody's dietary needs. Plus, suggestions are included for easy ingredient substitutions where applicable.

In addition to mouthwatering meals and lip-smacking treats, you'll find ideas for Harry Potter holiday-themed parties and suggested menus for Christmas Eve, Christmas Day, and Boxing Day along with ideas for a Slughorn-style cocktail party, a Yule Ball, and a Movie Night, among others, to bring about Christmas cheer. The recipes within this book will create unforgettable meals that will give friends, family, partygoers, and guests a very Happy Christmas!

BREAKFASTS

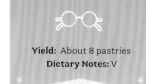

Yield: About 8 pastries
Dietary Notes: V

Restricted Section
PUFF PASTRY BOOKS

Over the Christmas holiday of their first year at Hogwarts, Hermione Granger tasks Harry Potter to enter the Restricted Section in the school's library to search for books on Sorcerer's Stone creator Nicolas Flamel. These scenes were filmed on location in the Tudor-era Duke Humfrey's Library at Oxford University, which chains its books to the shelves. The books in the Hogwarts Library are thick, heavy tomes that might scream at you when opened, as did the first one Harry looked into during his search. You'll scream in delight at these light and crunchy "books" made from puff pastry dough.

> "Good. You can help Harry, then. He's going to go and look in the library for information on Nicolas Flamel."
>
> "We've looked a hundred times!"
>
> "Not in the Restricted Section. Happy Christmas!"
>
> —Hermione Granger and Ron Weasley, *Harry Potter and the Sorcerer's Stone*

INGREDIENTS

One 17-ounce package puff pastry, thawed according to package directions

6 tablespoons unsalted butter, melted, divided

2 to 3 drops black food coloring

¼ cup sugar

½ teaspoon five-spice powder

1. Prepare a baking sheet with a silicone baking mat or parchment paper and make sure that the pastry is thawed.

2. Put 2 tablespoons of the melted butter in a small dish and add the food coloring, stir to combine. Have the remaining melted butter in another small dish with 2 pastry brushes. Mix the sugar with the five spice in a small bowl.

3. Working with 1 sheet of pastry at a time, roll it out to approximately 12 inches by 10 inches. Cut the sheet into 2-by-3-inch rectangles, creating 20 from each sheet. Use a 2-inch egg-shaped cookie cutter to cut an egg out of 4 of the rectangles.

4. Working on the prepared baking sheet, place 1 rectangle down, and brush it with the black butter mixture. Use a fork to prick the center of the rectangle to make about 4 rows of marks, and place another rectangle on top. Use the second pastry brush to brush this piece with the plain butter, sprinkle with the spiced sugar, and score the center again with the fork. Layer 2 more rectangles on top, brushing each with plain butter and sprinkling with more sugar. When you have a stack of 4 rectangles, take a chopstick and press it down in the center of the stack, across the short side, creating the center of the "book." Gently indent the top and bottom of the book by pinching with your fingers.

5. Paint the egg-shaped pieces with the black butter and use the tip of the chopstick to create eyes and a mouth. Place this in the center of the book, pressing gently to adhere. Repeat with the rest of the rectangles and the second sheet of pastry. Chill for 20 minutes in the refrigerator.

6. While the books are chilling, preheat the oven to 400°F.

7. Bake for 15 to 20 minutes or until golden brown and puffed. Serve warm or at room temperature. Store in an airtight container for up to 2 days.

Yield: About 4 cups
Dietary Notes: GF*, V, V+*

GRANOLA BREAKFAST
of Triwizard Champions

As we learn in *Harry Potter and the Goblet of Fire*, there are three tasks to be accomplished in the Triwizard Tournament: outwit a dragon, recover a "treasure" under the waters of the Black Lake, and navigate a dangerous maze in order to win the Triwizard Cup. And as it's said that breakfast is the most important meal of the day, then the tournament's four champions (Durmstrang Institute's Viktor Krum, Beauxbatons Academy's Fleur Delacour, and Hogwarts' Cedric Diggory and Harry Potter) would already be front-runners if they started their day with this healthy granola breakfast. Almonds and pecans offer endless energy, oats and flaxseed will fuel the whole body, and the delicious addition of fruits and spices make this a definite winner.

> "Now, for those of you who do not know, the Triwizard Tournament brings together three schools for a series of magical contests. From each school, a single student is selected to compete."
>
> —Albus Dumbledore,
> *Harry Potter and the Goblet of Fire*

INGREDIENTS

¼ cup coconut oil

¼ cup honey or agave

2 cups old fashioned oats

½ cup flaxseed

1 cup whole almonds

½ cup pecan pieces

1 teaspoon cinnamon

½ teaspoon ginger

1½ cups dried fruit combo of choice, such as golden raisins, currants, dried cherries, diced dried apricot and/or coconut flakes

1. Preheat the oven to 300°F. Line a large, rimmed baking sheet with parchment paper.

2. In a microwave-safe bowl, combine the coconut oil and honey. Heat for 1 minute, carefully remove from the microwave, and stir to combine.

3. In a large bowl, combine the oats, flaxseed, almonds, pecan pieces, cinnamon, and ginger. Stir together until well combined. Stir the coconut oil and honey into the oat mixture. Spread the mixture onto the baking sheet in an even layer and bake for 15 to 20 minutes, stirring occasionally, until the mixture is mostly dry and the nuts are well toasted.

4. Remove from the oven and stir in your desired dried fruit mixture. Allow to cool completely in the pan. Store in an airtight container for up to 1 month, or package into treat bags as gifts.

Note | This recipe can be made gluten free with gluten free oats and vegan by using agave instead of honey.

Snape's
BUBBLE AND SQUEAK

Bubble and Squeak, a classic British breakfast dish, was named for the sounds made by its ingredients when cooked which are reminiscent of the gurgles and shrieks made by something brewing in a cauldron in Potions class. Bubble and Squeak is a brilliant way to incorporate any leftovers from Christmas dinner—if there are any! You can mash up any surplus potatoes or root vegetables to use in the recipe. Boxing Day doesn't refer to the sport, but to the boxes of gifts given to those who attended other celebrations on Christmas, and this heartening dish is a gift in itself.

> **"Bubble, bubble, toil and trouble**
> **Fire burn and cauldron bubble."**
>
> —Frog Choir,
> *Harry Potter and the Prisoner of Azkaban*

INGREDIENTS

1½ pounds golden potatoes, peeled and cubed

¼ cup hazelnuts

2 tablespoon olive oil

6 tablespoons salted butter, divided

2 cups leftover roasted vegetables, such as Sprout's Superior Sprouts (page 45) or Quick Roasted Vegetables (page 74)

1. Bring a large pot of salted water to a boil over medium-high heat. Add the cubed potatoes and boil for 10 to 15 minutes or until potatoes are tender. Remove from heat and drain immediately.

2. In a large bowl, mix the hot potatoes with the leftover vegetables, stir to combine, and mash well with a wooden spoon or potato masher. Add the hazelnuts and stir again.

3. Add the olive oil and four tablespoons of the butter to a large skillet over medium heat. When the butter is foaming, add the vegetable mixture. Level out in the pan and cook for 10 minutes.

4. Use the flat edge of a wooden spoon to turn over the mixture, scraping up the brown bits from the bottom of the pan and mixing them in, mashing the vegetables a bit more as you go. Level out the mixture again and cook undisturbed for 10 minutes.

5. After the second 10 minutes, stir the mixture again, scraping up all the brown bits and stirring them in. Level the mixture out again, compacting it and shaping it into a thick patty.

6. Cook undisturbed for 20 minutes. Use a spatula to check the bottom to see if it's well browned. If ready, turn off the heat, cover the skillet with a large cutting board or platter and flip the patty out of the pan. Serve with fried or scrambled eggs.

Note | This recipe can be made vegetarian by using the Quick Roasted Vegetables instead of Sprout's Superior Sprouts.

The Christmas card—like snow-filled
streets of Hogsmeade as seen in *Harry Potter
and the Prisoners of Azkaban*.

Neville's
TOAD IN THE HOLE

Neville Longbottom is constantly losing his toad, Trevor. The warty creature wanders away on the Hogwarts Express before the first-year students enter the Great Hall for sorting in *Harry Potter and the Sorcerer's Stone*. Trevor the Toad, played by four different toads in the films, had a terrarium to rest in between takes. The last place he'd be found, however, is in this traditional English dish, as there is no record of toads ever being used in the recipe. The name is thought to come from the resemblance of the sausages to the way toads poke their heads out of their burrows.

> "Has anyone seen a toad? A boy named Neville's lost one."
>
> —Hermione Granger,
> *Harry Potter and the Sorcerer's Stone*

INGREDIENTS

For the Batter

1 cup milk

1 tablespoon Worcestershire sauce

1 teaspoon Dijon mustard

3 eggs

1 cup flour

¼ teaspoon salt

Fresh ground pepper to taste

For the Sausages

2 tablespoons vegetable oil

2 tablespoons roughly torn sage leaves

1 pound sausage links

1. Preheat the oven to 400°F. If possible, do not use a convection oven as sometimes the air flow will inhibit the rising of the Yorkshire pudding.

2. **To make the batter:** In a large measuring cup, whisk together the milk, Worcestershire sauce, mustard, and eggs until thoroughly combined. In a separate bowl, stir together flour, salt, and ground pepper. Whisk the egg mixture into the flour mixture until smooth. Set aside to rest.

3. **To make the sausages:** Put a medium cast iron skillet, or other high heat skillet, on the stove over medium-high heat. Add the vegetable oil, and when it starts to shimmer add the sage leaves and sausages. Turn the sausages until they brown on all sides, 2 to 3 minutes. Remove the pan from the heat and remove the sausages to a plate.

4. Pour the batter into the pan and place the sausages on the batter, leaving a bit of space in between each one. Place the skillet in the oven. Do not open the oven door for at least 20 minutes. Remove from the oven when dark golden brown and puffed. Serve immediately.

5. Pairs well with scrambled or fried eggs.

The Chosen One

TOAST LIGHTNING BOLTS WITH CODDLED EGGS

When Harry Potter—The Chosen One was an infant, the Dark wizard Lord Voldemort cast the *Avada Kedavra* curse at him, leaving the baby with a lightning bolt–shaped scar on the right side of his forehead. Over the course of the eight Harry Potter films, Harry's scar was applied to actor Daniel Radcliffe's forehead more than 2,000 times. These coddled eggs bring to mind the first time we see baby Harry in *Harry Potter and the Sorcerer's Stone* swaddled in a soft blanket when Dumbledore gently laid himdown on the Dursleys' door step. The toasted bread laid on top has its own lightning bolt shape upon it.

· INGREDIENTS ·

2 teaspoons salted butter, divided, plus more for bread

2 teaspoons shredded cheddar cheese

2 large eggs

1 tablespoon snipped chives

Fresh ground pepper to taste

Two pieces sliced bread

Specialty Tools

2 egg coddlers or low wide mouth mason jars

Large saucepan with tight-fitting lid and rack or folded tea towel

Lightning bolt–shaped cookie cutter

"Do you really have the . . . ?"

"The what?"

"The scar."

—Ron Weasley and Harry Potter,
Harry Potter and the Sorcerer's Stone

1. **To make the eggs:** Place the rack or folded tea towel inside the large saucepan and place the two empty coddlers or jars inside. Fill the pan with water until it reaches the bottom of the coddler lids. Remove coddlers from the saucepan and bring the water to a boil over medium-high heat.

2. While the water is boiling, use ½ teaspoon of butter on each jar to thoroughly grease the inside of each container. Split the cheese between the bottoms of each jar. Crack the eggs and gently add one to each jar. Top with an additional ½ teaspoon butter each and half the chives each. Add fresh ground pepper to taste.

3. Seal each jar or coddler tightly and once the water has reached a boil, place them inside the pot. Cover immediately and reduce heat to simmer over medium heat. Simmer 8 to 10 minutes or until eggs are set to desired firmness.

4. **To make the toast:** Butter the center of both sides of each slice of bread and cut two lightning bolts from each piece. Place in a hot skillet or on a hot griddle and toast each side to desired doneness. Serve each egg by placing each coddler and two lightning bolts on a salad plate and serve immediately.

Note | This recipe can be made gluten free by using gluten-free bread.

SOUPS & STARTERS

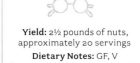

Yield: 2½ pounds of nuts,
approximately 20 servings
Dietary Notes: GF, V

Slug Club Christmas Party
SPICED NUTS

Professor Slughorn's exclusive Slug Club includes a collection of students who are gifted, favorites, or expected to go on to illustrious careers. One perk is the Christmas party he hosts, where he serves a variety of his favorite festive hors d'oeuvres: fruit spears, tiny taco shells cradling chopped veggies, pretzels, and bowls of nuts. This spiced nut version would fit perfectly at one of his parties and offers a bit of heat with peanuts, cashews, and pecans coated with cayenne pepper and garam masala, a warming Indian spice blend.

> **"Everyone, carry on! Carry on!"**
>
> —Horace Slughorn,
> *Harry Potter and the Half-Blood Prince*

INGREDIENTS

½ cup light brown sugar, firmly packed

1 tablespoon kosher salt

1 tablespoon cayenne pepper

½ tablespoon garam masala

2 egg whites or 4 tablespoons pasteurized egg whites

1 pound roasted, unsalted peanuts

1 pound roasted, unsalted cashews

½ pound roasted, unsalted pecan halves

1. Preheat the oven to 300°F and line two rimmed baking sheets with parchment paper.

2. In a large bowl, whisk together the sugar, salt, cayenne, and garam masala. Add the egg whites and whisk until completely combined and a thick paste forms.

3. Add the peanuts, cashews, and pecan halves, and stir until they are evenly coated. Spread out the mixture onto the prepared baking sheets in even, single layers. Bake for 25 to 30 minutes, rotating once halfway through, or until the mixture is dry and fragrant.

4. Allow to cool completely before storing in an airtight container for up to 1 week.

Tip | To help break up the nut clusters, roll them up in the parchment while still on the baking sheet.

Yield: 12 deviled eggs
Dietary Notes: GF, V

Bubbling Cauldron
BITES

These cauldron-shaped egg bites "bubble" with chives, peas, and horseradish cream, a concoction any potions maker would be proud to produce. For the films, prop makers created more than 200 cauldrons for use in the Potions classes. For Professor Slughorn's classes, three bespoke cauldrons were created in which to hold the potions the professor tests his students with. Hermione Granger identifies the three: one contains Veritaserum, the truth-telling serum; the next is filled with Polyjuice Potion. Then she identifies the love potion Amortentia, which gives off scents unique to the user. The scents she smells that waft up from that particular cauldron are colored green for "freshly mown grass," white for "parchment," and green and orange for "spearmint toothpaste."

> **"All students must be equipped with . . . one standard size two pewter cauldron . . ."**
>
> —Hogwarts Invitation Letter,
> *Harry Potter and the Sorcerer's Stone*

Continued on page 26

Continued from page 25

INGREDIENTS

6 eggs

½ cup rice
wine vinegar

3 to 4 drops
black food coloring

½ cup cooked
English peas

¼ cup crème fraîche

1 teaspoon
horseradish cream

1 tablespoon snipped
chives, plus
more for garnish

¼ teaspoon salt

¼ teaspoon
garlic powder

Flat ended toothpicks,
optional

Note | The eggs can be made up to 1 day ahead. Store the egg whites and filling in separate containers and assemble just before serving.

1. **To boil the eggs:** Fill a large pot, big enough to hold the eggs in a layer, with cold water, until it just covers the eggs. Place the pot on the stove over medium-high heat, cover, and bring to a boil. As soon as the water boils, remove the pan from the heat, leave covered, and let sit for 5 to 6 minutes depending on how firm you like your yolks. While the eggs are cooking, prepare an ice bath in a large bowl. When the eggs are done, submerge them into the ice bath and leave for 2 or 3 minutes. Peel the boiled eggs.

2. Alternatively, you can use your preferred cooking method or use store-bought hard-boiled eggs.

3. Cut each egg in half across the middle, along the short side. With a paring knife, carefully remove a sliver of egg white so that each half will sit upright.

4. Remove the egg yolk from each half and store in an airtight container in the refrigerator.

5. Combine the rice wine vinegar and food coloring with 3 cups water in a container large enough to hold the eggs in a single layer. Add the egg whites to the container and push each one down so it fills with the dye and place a piece of parchment paper over the top to help them stay submerged. Let the eggs soak in the dye for 5 to 10 minutes until the desired color is reached. They should start to resemble small cauldrons.

6. Line a baking sheet with a few layers of paper towel and use a slotted spoon to remove the eggs from the dye, place them open side down, and let them dry while you make the filling.

7. To the bowl of a food processor, add the cooked peas, crème fraîche, horseradish cream, chives, salt, and garlic powder. Run the processor until the mixture is mostly smooth, about 1 minute. Add the egg yolks and run the processor again for about 30 seconds or until the egg yolks have been incorporated.

8. Set each egg white upright and use a small spoon or cookie scoop to fill each egg with a mounded tablespoon of filling. Garnish with more snipped chives and add a toothpick "spoon" if desired. Serve immediately.

Swedish Short-Snout's
STEAK TARTARE

Among the variety of starters for Horace Slughorn's Slug Club Christmas Party is a tartare that, unfortunately, does horrible things to one's breath once eaten. (Hermione gobbles some up to keep Cormac McLaggen's unwanted advances at bay.) Inspired by—but not tasting like—that questionable hors d'oeuvre is this tartare featuring filet mignon. This version is great for heating up in cold weather with a blend of red pepper flakes and wasabi paste in its mix. Even a dragon would enjoy its fiery flavors.

> **"Marvelous creatures,
> dragons, aren't they?"**
>
> —Alastor "Mad-Eye" Moody,
> *Harry Potter and the Goblet of Fire*

INGREDIENTS

8-ounce filet mignon

2 tablespoons finely minced shallot

½ teaspoon red pepper flakes

½ teaspoon wasabi paste

1 teaspoon lemon zest

1 teaspoon kosher salt

1½ teaspoons rice wine vinegar

1 egg yolk, room temperature

2 tablespoons olive oil

Toasted baguette slices or crackers, for serving

1. Cut the beef into 1-inch cubes, cleaning it of any fat or membrane. Place it on a plate and freeze it for 10 minutes.

2. While the beef is in the freezer, in a medium bowl, combine the shallot, red pepper flakes, wasabi paste, lemon zest, salt, rice wine vinegar, and egg yolk. Whisk until blended. Slowly drizzle in the olive oil, whisking as you go, until the dressing comes together.

3. Remove the beef from the freezer and, in small batches, mince it into very small pieces. Fold the beef into the dressing and serve immediately with toasted baguette or crackers.

Note | This recipe can be made gluten-free by serving with a gluten-free baguette or crackers.

Yule Ball
COCKTAIL SHRIMP

For the Yule Ball's holiday feast seen in *Harry Potter and the Goblet of Fire*, set decorator Stephenie McMillan decided they should have seafood, served cold on an icy base, complementing the wintry celebration. The Yule Ball was a special occasion for many reasons. It was here Hermione Granger made a fashion statement in a pink ombre dress created from thirty-nine feet of chiffon and silk and a statement in fact that if Ron was jealous of her date, he should have asked her first!

> **"The Yule Ball has been a tradition of the Triwizard Tournament since its inception."**
>
> —Minerva McGonagall,
> *Harry Potter and the Goblet of Fire*

INGREDIENTS

For the Sauce
1 cup Greek yogurt
¼ cup mayonnaise
1 teaspoon curry powder
½ teaspoon salt
¼ teaspoon cayenne pepper

For the Shrimp
1 pound (16 to 20 count) whole shrimp

4 cups low sodium vegetable broth

1 small lemon, cut in half, plus 2 more, cut into wedges, for garnish

2 bay leaves

1 tablespoon whole peppercorns

2 cloves garlic, peeled and smashed

1. **To make the sauce:** In a 2-cup airtight container, mix together the Greek yogurt, mayonnaise, curry powder, salt, and cayenne. Cover, and refrigerate at least 30 minutes, or until ready to serve, to let the flavor develop.

2. **To make the shrimp:** Use kitchen shears to cut along the back of the shrimp, leaving the tail intact, and devein. Leave the shells on.

3. In a large pot over medium-high heat, add the vegetable broth, lemon halves, bay leaves, peppercorns, and garlic cloves. Bring to a boil, turn the heat down to medium-low, add the shrimp and cover. Simmer for 3 to 5 minutes or until the shrimp are pink and opaque.

4. Use tongs to move the shrimp to a platter. When cool enough to handle, peel and then chill for at least 30 minutes before serving. Shrimp can be made up to 1 day ahead, refrigerated in an airtight container.

5. When ready to serve, put the sauce in a small bowl in the center of a platter surrounded by shrimp Garnish with lemon wedges.

Slughorn's Appetizer
ROLL-UPS

For his Slug Club Christmas get-together, Horace Slughorn chose to match the party's decorations to the muted red and green tones of the professor's tasseled paisley robe. The space was a redecoration of the Room of Requirement set, whose columns were concealed with layers of a shot silk fabric in jade green. Among the dishes on the red-covered tables are platters of sushi, wrapped in green nori, which gives the effect of Christmas colors.

> **"In the old days, I used to throw together the occasional supper party. Select student or two. Would you be game?"**
>
> —Horace Slughorn,
> *Harry Potter and the Half-Blood Prince*

INGREDIENTS

2 cups uncooked sushi rice

2 teaspoons rice wine vinegar

1 teaspoon salt

4 ounces lump crab meat or cooked shrimp meat, chopped

1 tablespoon mayonnaise

½ teaspoon sriracha

1 teaspoon dried chives

½ teaspoon onion powder

4 sheets of nori

2 small Persian cucumbers, julienned

½ avocado, sliced thin

2 teaspoons capers

Specialty Tools
Sushi mat

1. Cook the sushi rice using a rice cooker or according to the package directions. When the rice is cooked, use a rice paddle or flat wooden spoon to spread it out on a baking sheet, sprinkle with the rice wine vinegar and salt, and use the paddle to gently fold it in. Once seasoned, spread it out again and set aside.

2. Mix the crab or shrimp with the mayonnaise, sriracha, chives, and onion powder.

3. Working with one sheet of nori at a time, lay the sheet on the sushi mat with a long side facing you. Use slightly damp hands to spread about ¾ cup rice onto the nori sheet, covering it from edge to edge, leaving a ¾-inch border on the edge farthest from you. Place half the seafood mixture down the center of the rice. Roll the mat away from you once, pressing the filling to create a firm roll. Lift the top of the mat and use your finger to press the clean edge of nori onto the roll. Cover with the mat and roll once more to further tighten the roll. Remove from the mat and set aside.

4. Repeat these steps, first with the remaining seafood, creating a total of 2 rolls, then with the remaining two using half the cucumber, avocado, and 1 teaspoon capers for each roll. When all the rolls are made use a very sharp knife to cut 8 equal pieces from each roll. Arrange on a platter and serve immediately.

5. Serve with a small dish of soy sauce if desired.

Note | The filling can be adjusted as needed for either both seafood options, all vegetarian, or get creative and choose your own. Smoked salmon, thinly sliced cooked beef, or tobiko make great options.

In *Harry Potter and the Chamber of Secrets*, sleighs race over the frozen lake at Christmastime in concept art by Adam Brockbank.

Nicolas Flamel
VICHYSSOISE SOUP

Nicolas Flamel is a 665-year-old French alchemist at the time of *Harry Potter and the Sorcerer's Stone* and the only known maker of the titular stone itself. Vichyssoise is an American version of a classic French potato-and-leek soup, served cold instead of hot. Though there is only one stone, the prop makers for the film designed several, made out of a molded resin in a rich ruby red. Harry was surprised to find the stone in his pocket, and you'll be surprised to find a red roasted tomato at the bottom of your bowl the same color as the Sorcerer's Stone.

INGREDIENTS

For the Vichyssoise
4 large leeks

3 tablespoons unsalted butter

1 tablespoon olive oil

1 teaspoon kosher salt, plus more for seasoning

1 pound golden potatoes, peeled and cubed

5 cups vegetable broth

1 cup heavy cream

½ teaspoon ground white pepper

For the Sorcerer's Stone Tomatoes
6 Campari tomatoes

1 tablespoon olive oil

Up to 1 teaspoon salt

"The only stone currently in existence belongs to Mr. Nicolas Flamel, who last year celebrated his 665th birthday."

—Hermione Granger,
Harry Potter and the Sorcerer's Stone

1. **To make the soup:** Slice the white and light green parts of the leeks thinly, add to a large colander, and rinse well.

2. In a large pot over medium heat, combine the butter, olive oil, and 1 teaspoon salt. When the butter is completely melted, add the leeks. Cook, stirring frequently, until softened but not brown, 10 to 15 minutes.

3. Add the potatoes and stir to coat, then add the vegetable broth. Increase the heat to medium-high, bring to a low boil, then reduce to a simmer, over low heat. Simmer for 30 minutes or until potatoes are very tender.

4. Remove from the heat and use an immersion blender to purée until completely smooth, 2 to 3 minutes. Add the heavy cream, white pepper, and more salt to taste.

5. **To make the Sorcerer's Stone tomatoes:** While the soup is simmering, preheat oven to 400°F.

6. Place the tomatoes stem side down on a rimmed baking sheet and coat with the olive oil. Roast for 10 to 15 minutes or until softened and split. Sprinkle each tomato with a pinch of salt.

7. To serve, place one tomato in the bottom of a low, wide, soup bowl and ladle soup over it.

Note | Vichyssoise soup can be served hot or cold. Leftovers can be stored in an airtight container for up to 3 days. Roasted tomatoes can be stored in a separate container for up to 3 days.

Yield: About 12 cups
or 8 servings
Dietary Notes: GF, V, V+

Hagrid's
ONE-POT PUMPKIN STEW

Behind Hagrid's hut is a lush pumpkin patch, the perfect place to find the main ingredient for this nourishing stew, filled with the best of winter's vegetables. The patch was one place his Hippogriff, Buckbeak, rested and where he might have nipped at the vegetables as they grew. The scenes of the pumpkin patch in *Harry Potter and the Prisoner of Azkaban* were filmed on a hillside in the Scottish Highlands. The sitting animatronic Buckbeak was mounted on rails over the muddy turf, as it rained most days while they were shooting. A stew like this one is a great way to brighten up your day, regardless of the weather.

> **"There's no Hogwarts
> without you, Hagrid."**
>
> —Harry Potter,
> *Harry Potter and the Prisoner of Azkaban*

INGREDIENTS

- 1 bunch rainbow chard
- 1 tablespoon harissa powder
- One 15-ounce can chickpeas, drained
- 2 tablespoons olive oil
- 1 yellow onion, diced
- 2 red bell peppers, cored, deseeded, and diced
- 2 teaspoons salt
- 6 cups vegetable broth
- One 6-ounce can tomato paste
- 1½ to 2 pounds pumpkin or winter squash, such as winter luxury, kabocha, or Jarrahdale

1. Tear the leaves from the stems of the chard and set the leaves aside. Rinse the stems and finely dice.
2. In a large pot over medium-high heat, add the harissa powder and the chickpeas. Cook for 2 to 3 minutes stirring constantly until the harissa is fragrant and the chickpeas have dried out.
3. Add the olive oil, stir to coat, and then add the onion, bell pepper, and chard stems. Sauté 2 to 3 minutes more until the onion begins to soften. Add the salt and continue cooking another 3 to 4 minutes until the vegetables release their juices and deglaze the bottom of the pan.
4. Add in the vegetable broth and the tomato paste. Stir to combine. Add in the pumpkin chunks and simmer the stew for 20 to 30 minutes or until the pumpkin is tender.
5. When ready to serve, rinse the chard leaves, roughly chop, stir into the soup, and let cook for 1 minute. Serve immediately.
6. Stew can be made up to a day ahead and should be refrigerated in an airtight container until serving.

Note | If making the stew ahead, leave the chard leaves out until ready to serve. Reheat the soup, add the leaves, stir, and let cook for 1 minute.

Yield: About 4 cups
or 4 servings
Dietary Notes: GF*, V, V+*

Leaky Cauldron's
ROASTED TOMATO SOUP
with Marmite Grilled Cheese

A warming roasted tomato soup served with a Marmite grilled cheese sandwich is an iconic British meal that could have been served at The Leaky Cauldron. After all, when you have a cauldron as inspiration, soups are a given. On a sign created by the graphics department for *Harry Potter and the Sorcerer's Stone*, there are several soups offered, including Leaky House Soup, Soup Leaky House, and House Soup Leaky. This rich tomato soup is accompanied by a grilled cheese sandwich prepared with Marmite, a popular British toast topping, a savory food spread made from the yeasty byproducts of beer brewing.

INGREDIENTS

For the Soup

2 pounds Roma tomatoes

2 tablespoons olive oil, divided

1 teaspoon kosher salt

1 yellow onion, roughly chopped

3 cloves garlic, peeled and smashed

¼ cup balsamic vinegar

2 cups vegetable broth

½ cup unsweetened oat milk

For the Sandwiches

8 slices white or buttermilk bread

3 tablespoons unsalted butter

4 teaspoons Marmite

6 ounces English cheddar, finely grated

> **"Leaky Cauldron! Stay away from the pea soup!"**
>
> —Shrunken head on the Knight Bus, *Harry Potter and the Prisoner of Azkaban*

1. **To make the soup:** Preheat the oven to 450°F with the rack in the upper third of the oven.

2. Cut the tomatoes in half and remove most of the core and seeds. Place cut side down on a rimmed baking sheet and coat with 1 tablespoon of the olive oil and the salt. Roast for 15 to 20 minutes, or until the skin is blistered and the tomatoes are softened.

3. While the tomatoes are roasting, heat a medium soup pot over medium-high heat with the remaining tablespoon of olive oil. Add the onions and garlic and cook, stirring frequently, until onions are completely soft and starting to brown, 7 to 10 minutes.

4. Add the balsamic vinegar and use it to deglaze the bottom of the pan. Reduce the heat to low and simmer the onions until most of the liquid has reduced.

5. Add the roasted tomatoes and vegetable broth and simmer for 15 to 20 minutes until the garlic cloves are very soft and the mixture has thickened slightly.

6. Purée with an immersion blender until very smooth, about 3 minutes. Add the oat milk and stir.

7. Soup should be served immediately or stored in an airtight container in the refrigerator for up to 3 days.

Note | If you don't have an immersion blender, allow the soup to cool for 30 minutes. Carefully blend in a blender until smooth. Reheat and stir in oat milk.

8. **To make the sandwiches:** Cut the crusts off all the bread slices. Spread ½ the butter evenly across one side of each piece and toast in a large skillet on medium-high heat until golden brown.

9. Remove from the pan and spread each buttered side with about 1 teaspoon Marmite per sandwich.

10. Place about 1½ ounces cheddar cheese on one Marmite side. Top with another piece of bread Marmite side down. Use the rest of the butter to butter the outsides of each sandwich. Place the sandwiches, one or two at a time, in the pan and grill until each side is golden brown, about 2 minutes per side.

11. Cut each sandwich in half and serve immediately with a bowl of hot soup.

Note | This recipe can be made vegan by using a plant-based spread and cheese. Use gluten-free bread for a gluten-free option.

BREADS & SIDES

The Burrow
WELCOME WREATH

In *Harry Potter and the Half-Blood Prince*, Harry spends Christmas with the Weasley family at The Burrow, their intricately constructed home. The redheaded family has always given Harry the warmest of welcomes. "The Weasleys are really the only family Harry's got in terms of love and friendship," says Julie Walters, who plays the Weasley matriarch, Molly. The love between family members is apparent (although Percy is sometimes on the out) and it's not surprising that they open their home at the holidays to all. This edible Christmas wreath with roasted red pepper "berries" sends a doughy, pesto holiday greeting to all.

> "It's not much, but it's home."
>
> "I think it's brilliant."
>
> —Ron Weasley and Harry Potter,
> *Harry Potter and the Chamber of Secrets*

Continued on page 44

Continued from page 43

1. **To make the dough:** Combine the milk, sugar, and yeast in a small bowl. Stir and set aside until foamy, about 5 minutes.

2. While the yeast is activating, put the flour, olive oil, egg, and salt in the bowl of a stand mixer fitted with a dough hook attachment. Mix on low briefly to combine.

3. Once the yeast is foamy, add it to the stand mixer and mix on low until the dough comes together, about 5 minutes. If the dough is too moist, add 1 tablespoon of flour at a time until it just comes together. Once the dough pulls away from the side of the bowl, continue to knead it with the dough hook for another 5 minutes, until elastic.

4. Place the dough in a large oiled bowl. Cover with a clean towel and let rise for 1 to 1½ hours or until it has doubled in size and is puffy when touched.

5. **While the dough is rising, make the pesto:** Add the walnuts to the bowl of a food processor and pulse 2 to 3 times. Add the arugula and basil leaves and pulse again until well chopped. Add the garlic powder, salt, and olive oil and run the processor until a thick paste has formed, up to 1 minute. Scrape into an airtight container and refrigerate until needed.

6. **To assemble:** Line a baking sheet with a silicone baking mat or pachment.

7. Once the dough has risen, roll it out on a lightly floured surface to an approximately 10-by-20-inch rectangle. Brush the surface with the tablespoon of olive oil and spread the pesto mixture evenly over the surface. Sprinkle the grated parmesan cheese evenly over the pesto.

8. Starting from a long edge, begin to roll a tight roll, and pinch the ends closed. Use a sharp knife to cut the roll in half lengthwise. With the filling facing upward twist the two pieces together overlapping alternately, as if you were creating a braid.

9. Gently lift the braid onto the baking sheet and form into a circular wreath. Pinch the ends together to close. Pick up any loose filling and sprinkle it back over the wreath using it to cover any exposed dough, especially toward the pinched ends. Cover with greased plastic wrap and allow to proof while you preheat the oven to 400°F for 15 minutes. Bake for 25 to 30 minutes or until golden brown. Allow to cool at least 15 minutes before decorating and serving. If decorating, stuff each cherry pepper with a mozzarella ball to "inflate" and pin onto the wreath with toothpicks. Tuck the arugula leaves off to one side.

INGREDIENTS

For the Dough
¾ cup whole milk, warmed to 110°F

1 tablespoon sugar

1 packet (2¼ teaspoons) instant yeast

3 cups all-purpose flour

3 tablespoons olive oil, plus more for oiling the bowl

1 egg

1 teaspoon kosher salt

For the Pesto
½ cup walnut pieces

1 cup baby arugula leaves (also called rocket)

½ cup basil leaves

¼ teaspoongarlic powder

½ teaspoon kosher salt

2 teaspoons olive oil

For the Wreath Assembly
1 tablespoon olive oil

½ cup grated parmesan cheese

2 pickled cherry peppers, optional

2 Ciliegine mozzarella balls, optional

2 arugula leaves, optional

Note | You can stuff extra peppers with more mozzarella balls and serve in a bowl alongside the bread.

Yield: 6 servings
Dietary Notes: GF

Sprout's Superior
SPROUTS

Professor Pomona Sprout teaches Herbology at Hogwarts in greenhouses filled with plants of all kinds, which provide ingredients for potions and draughts. Some plants, more than likely, are tasty and nutritional, like the Brussels sprouts in this recipe. To ensure your Brussels sprouts are as superior as Professor Sprout's, remove the thicker outer leaves, which are usually more bitter than other parts of the plant. You should also wash the sprouts to remove any dirt that may be left. In this recipe, bacon offers a splash of salt and dried cranberries add a smidge of sweetness.

> **"Welcome to Greenhouse Three, second years."**
>
> —Pomona Sprout,
> *Harry Potter and the Chamber of Secrets*

INGREDIENTS

- 1 pound Brussels sprouts
- 4 pieces of bacon, diced
- 1 tablespoon olive oil
- ¼ cup dried cranberries
- ½ teaspoon salt

1. Preheat the oven to 375°F.

2. Remove the tough or bruised guard leaves from each Brussels sprout. Rinse the Brussels sprouts in a colander and drain. Cut the tough stem off each one and then cut in half. Set aside.

3. Scatter bacon pieces on a rimmed baking sheet and bake for 7 minutes, then remove the baking sheet from the oven. Add the Brussels sprouts and shake to coat with the bacon pieces. Drizzle with the olive oil. Make sure all the Brussels sprouts are lying cut side down in a single layer. Roast for another 10 to 15 minutes or until the Brussels sprouts are well browned on the cut edge and tender.

4. Toss with the cranberries and salt. Serve immediately. Save any leftovers in an airtight container and use to make Snape's Bubble and Squeak (page 13).

The Great Hall covered in silver and ice for the
Yule Ball. Concept art by Adam Brockbank for
Harry Potter and the Goblet of Fire.

Grimmauld Place
DINNER ROLLS

In *Harry Potter and the Order of the Phoenix*, the Weasley family, Harry, and Hermione celebrate Christmas at Number Twelve, Grimmauld Place, the headquarters of the Order of the Phoenix and Sirius Black's ancestral home. A classic holiday spread is prepared, including a plate of rolls—inspiration for this dish—set beside a platter of turkey and potatoes on the long kitchen table. The Black family's twenty-foot-long kitchen table was handcrafted specifically for the film as tables that long are hard to find! These dinner rolls will also be hard to find once guests bite into these hot and tender baked breads.

> "Oh, Harry! There you are.
> Happy Christmas!"
>
> —Molly Weasley,
> *Harry Potter and the Order of the Phoenix*

INGREDIENTS

½ cup whole milk, warmed to 110°F

1 tablespoon honey

One packet (2¼ teaspoons) instant yeast

5 cups all-purpose flour

One 15-ounce can plain pumpkin purée

4 tablespoons unsalted butter, softened, plus more for serving

1 egg

2 teaspoons kosher salt

2 teaspoons paprika

1 teaspoon dried rosemary, divided

Egg wash (1 egg whisked with 1 tablespoon water)

2 teaspoons flake salt, optional

1. In a small bowl or measuring cup, combine the warmed milk, honey, and yeast. Stir to combine and set aside until the yeast is foaming, about 5 minutes.

2. In the bowl of a stand mixer fitted with a dough hook, combine the flour, pumpkin purée, butter, egg, salt, paprika, and ½ teaspoon of dried rosemary. Mix briefly to combine and then add the yeast and milk mixture and continue to mix.

3. Once a shaggy dough forms, stop the mixer and scrape down the sides of the bowl. Continue to knead with the dough hook on low for 5 minutes. Once the dough pulls away from the side of the bowl and becomes elastic, transfer it to a large oiled bowl, cover with a clean towel, and let rise for 1 to 1½ hours, or until the dough has doubled in size.

4. While the dough is rising, line 2 baking sheets with a silicone baking mat or parchment paper.

5. Working on a lightly floured surface, separate the dough into 16 equal portions. Working with one portion at a time and lightly floured hands, roll the dough out into a long snake, about 16 inches in length. Create a knot by forming a loose circle, in one hand, with a long tail. Use the other hand to feed the tail in and out of the circle and bring the end up through the middle. Place each finished knot on a prepared sheet. Allow to proof until they are puffy, about 1 hour. Toward the end of proofing, preheat the oven to 375°F.

6. Before the rolls go in the oven, brush each one with the egg wash and sprinkle with a few leaves of the remaining dried rosemary. Bake until golden brown and the internal temp reaches 190°F. Remove from the oven and sprinkle each roll with a pinch of flake salt, if using. Serve warm with more softened butter.

Yield: 6 servings
Dietary Notes: GF, V, V+*

Sirius
BLACK HEARTH POTATOES

Messages in the wizarding world can be sent by owl post, by Patronus, and by portraits. But what about a face-to-face conversation through the coals of a fireplace? Yes, that's possible, too. Harry Potter and Sirius Black have one such exchange in the Gryffindor common room's massive fireplace during the winter in *Harry Potter and the Goblet of Fire.* The common room was the first warm, comforting experience Harry has had outside his cupboard under the stairs, and these potatoes are also as comforting as time spent relaxing on the plush red couches in front of the common room's blazing fire. These delicious, tender potatoes are completely covered in a combination of black lava salt and kosher salt, then baked in a cast iron skillet to emerge from an ashy crust.

> "**Meet me in the Gryffindor common room at one o'clock this Saturday night.**"
>
> —Letter from Sirius Black,
> *Harry Potter and the Goblet of Fire*

INGREDIENTS

1½ pounds new or fingerling potatoes

2 cups kosher salt, divided

2 sprigs rosemary

¼ cup black salt

2 tablespoons unsalted butter, optional

1. Preheat the oven to 375°F.
2. Wash the potatoes well and dry them.
3. In a cast iron or ovenproof skillet, make a base layer of one cup salt. Arrange the potatoes in a single layer on top of the salt layer. Tuck in the two sprigs of rosemary around the edge of the pan.
4. Mix the remaining cup salt with the black salt. Pour the salt mixture evenly over the potatoes. They should be mostly covered but not necessarily completely covered.
5. Bake for 45 minutes to 1 hour or until the skins on the potatoes are puffed and the potatoes are fork tender.
6. Use a fork or tongs to remove potatoes from the salt. Serve as is or toss with 2 tablespoons unsalted butter.

Note | Once the salt has cooled, it can be saved to bake more potatoes, to serve as pie weights, or to use as a scrub for pots and pans. This recipe is easily made vegan by omitting the butter.

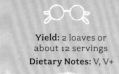

Yield: 2 loaves or about 12 servings

Dietary Notes: V, V+

Weasley Sweater
FOCACCIA

Given that the set designer and prop makers considered the Weasleys' home to be drafty, it's not surprising that Molly Weasley knits a lot of clothing for her family. And at Christmastime, it's likely her gifts will be made by her crafty hands. Over time, each of her children has received a sweater with their initial on the front, as seen in *Harry Potter and the Sorcerer's Stone*. Harry gets one as well during his first year at Hogwarts. These Italian flatbreads, called focaccia, have monogram toppings for Harry and Ron baked in, but feel free to get creative and add your own monogram.

> "What are you wearing?"
>
> "Oh, my mum made it. Looks like you've got one, too!"
>
> —Harry Potter and Ron Weasley,
> *Harry Potter and the Sorcerer's Stone*

Continued on page 54

Continued from page 53

1. In a medium bowl or measuring cup, combine the water, sugar, and yeast. Set aside until foamy, about 5 minutes.

2. In a large bowl, combine the flour and salt. Once the yeast is foamy, add it to the flour mixture and use a rubber spatula to stir it until no dry flour remains and a shaggy dough has formed.

3. Pour 4 tablespoons of the olive oil into a very large bowl, add the dough, and turn it 2 or 3 times to coat it with olive oil. Cover with a clean tea towel or plastic wrap. At this point the dough can either go in the refrigerator overnight, or to a warm place for 4 hours. The dough is ready when it has doubled in size.

4. When the dough is ready, deflate it by keeping the dough in the bowl and using two forks to flip the edge farthest from you toward you. Turn the bowl a quarter turn and repeat this step. Turn the bowl two more times, using the forks to flip the dough each time. You should be creating a rough ball.

5. Pour 2 tablespoons olive oil onto each sheet pan, or 4 on the larger pan, if using, and turn and tilt the pans to coat with the oil. Split the dough in half, and place on the baking sheets. Pour any remaining olive oil from the bowl onto each loaf. Let the dough proof in a warm place until doubled in size, about 1½ hours. It is ready when an indent, made with the tip of your finger, bounces back slowly and leaves a mark. If it bounces back quickly it needs more time. Toward the end of proofing, preheat the oven to 450°F.

6. When the dough is done proofing, gently push it to the edges of the pans with your fingers and then make dimples all over with the tips of your fingers.

7. Decorate with the vegetables and/or fruit creating an R monogram in the center of one loaf and an H monogram in the center of the other (or whatever monogram you'd like). Drizzle each with 1 tablespoon olive oil, and sprinkle with ½ teaspoon of flake salt, if using. Bake for 25 to 30 minutes or until golden brown all over and crisp at the edges. Serve warm. Leftovers can be stored in an airtight container for up to 3 days.

INGREDIENTS

2½ cups water, warmed to 110°F

2 teaspoons sugar

1 packet (2¼ teaspoons) instant yeast

5 cups all-purpose flour

1 tablespoon kosher salt

½ cup plus 2 tablespoons olive oil, divided

4 cups berries or diced vegetables (see note)

1 teaspoon flake salt, optional

Specialty Tools
Two 9-by-13-inch (or one 17-by-13-inch) rimmed baking sheets

Note | Bell peppers, green onions, red onions, shallots, or finely diced carrots work well as vegetable décor. Sliced strawberries, blueberries, raspberries, or thinly sliced pears work well for fruit options. Make sure to use a good quality olive oil that you love the taste of because it will feature prominently in the final product.

Hogwarts
YORKSHIRE PUDDING

As there are four houses at Hogwarts School of Witchcraft and Wizardry, there are four ingredients needed to make the traditional British Yorkshire pudding: eggs, flour, milk, and some form of fat that can range from oil to beef drippings. In Britain, "pudding" is synonymous with dessert, but can also refer to cakelike dishes such as this crispy puffed bread. Yorkshire puddings originated from York in Northern England.

> "Welcome, welcome to another year at Hogwarts. Now, I'd like to say a few words before we all become too befuddled by our excellent feast."
>
> —Albus Dumbledore,
> *Harry Potter and the Prisoner of Azkaban*

Note | Pan drippings from roast beef are a classic for Yorkshire Pudding but if your drippings fall short of ¼ cup, you can top them off with a high heat oil or replace the beef drippings altogether for a vegetarian option.

INGREDIENTS

4 eggs

1 cup whole milk

½ teaspoon salt

1 cup all-purpose flour

¼ cup pan drippings from roast beef (or high temperature oil, such as grape seed or avocado oil) (see note)

1. Add the eggs to a large bowl and whisk thoroughly. Add the milk and salt and whisk again. Add the flour all at once and whisk vigorously until no lumps remain and the batter is smooth, up to 3 minutes. Let the batter rest for at least 30 minutes.

2. Preheat the oven to 450°F.

3. Place 1 teaspoon of pan drippings into each cavity of a muffin or popover tin. Heat the pan and oil in the oven for 10 minutes. While the pan is heating, transfer the batter to a container with a pour spout.

4. Remove the pan from the oven. Pour the batter over a spoon to prevent splashing and fill each cavity ⅔ full. Bake for 20 to 25 minutes or until golden brown and crisp. Do not open the oven while baking until at least 20 minutes has gone by, as this may prevent rising. If possible do not use convection as this may prevent rising.

MAINS

Greenhouse Greens
SALAD

In *Harry Potter and the Chamber of Secrets*, second-year students file into Greenhouse Three for their first Herbology lesson, in which Professor Pomona Sprout teaches them how to repot the problematic, screaming baby Mandrakes. More than fifty animatronic Mandrakes were created for the scene, squirming and wriggling in their pots via controllers who sat under the Greenhouse's massively long trestle table. It's much less difficult to make this mouthwatering salad for a hearty dinner, which combines a crop of wintry vegetables including squash and rainbow carrots, plus fruity pomegranates, for a burst of color and lip-smacking flavor.

> **"Professor Sprout tells me you have an aptitude for Herbology."**
>
> —Alastor Moody to Neville Longbottom,
> *Harry Potter and the Goblet of Fire*

Note | This recipe can be made vegan by substituting maple syrup or agave for the honey.

INGREDIENTS

For the Salad
1 delicata squash
2 teaspoons olive oil
2 rainbow carrots, peeled
1 cucumber, peeled
4 radishes, cleaned and sliced thin
¼ cup pomegranate seeds
1 cup cherry tomatoes (preferably sun golds)

1 cup dry quinoa, cooked according to package directions
½ cup walnuts
5 ounces spring mix lettuce

For the Dressing
½ cup olive oil
¼ balsamic vinegar
½ teaspoon kosher salt
½ tablespoon Dijon mustard
1 tablespoon honey
¼ cup finely minced shallot

1. **To make the salad:** Preheat the oven to 400°F.

2. Cut the delicata squash in half lengthwise and scrape out the seeds and pulp. Cut each half into ½-inch slices, creating crescent moons.

3. Place the slices on a rimmed baking sheet and toss with the olive oil. Roast for 10 to 15 minutes, or until tender and browning. Allow to cool on the baking sheet while making the rest of the salad.

4. While the squash is roasting make the dressing: In a medium bowl or measuring cup, add the olive oil, vinegar, salt, mustard, honey, and shallot. Whisk until the dressing emulsifies. Set aside until ready to dress the salad.

5. **To assemble the salad:** Have a large salad bowl standing by. Use a vegetable peeler to cut wide ribbons of carrot into the salad. Stop when you reach the core of the carrot and save for a soup stock or discard.

6. Cut the cucumber in half lengthwise and scrape the seeds out with a spoon. Cut into ½-inch slices, and add them to the bowl.

7. Add the radishes, pomegranate seeds, tomatoes, walnuts, cooled squash, and quinoa. Toss all the ingredients together with the dressing, giving it a quick whisk again if needed. Add the spring mix and toss again. Served within 1 hour.

Yield: 6 servings
Dietary Notes: GF, V

Vegetarian

Madam Pomfrey's Hospitality
SHEPHERD'S PIE

Madam Poppy Pomfrey is the matron at Hogwarts, the "school nurse" who offers kindness to injured or bespelled students, whether they need to regrow bones, be restored from being Petrified by a Basilisk, or have been bitten by a possible Grim. Though she's no-nonsense, Madam Pomfrey is also gentle and calming, like the best comfort food. Shepherd's Pie is a traditional Irish dish that dates back to the 1700s. It's typically made with meat, but it's the simmered leeks, onions, mushrooms, and roasted cashews topped by fluffy mashed potatoes that give this its cozy flavor.

INGREDIENTS

For the Mashed Potatoes
2½ pounds gold potatoes, peeled and cubed

4 ounces cream cheese

4 tablespoons salted butter

1 teaspoon salt

Fresh ground pepper to taste

For the Filling
2 cups vegetable broth

1 cup roasted unsalted cashews

2 tablespoons vegetable oil

4 tablespoons salted butter

1 small leek, thinly sliced

1 small yellow onion, diced

8 ounces cremini mushrooms, thinly sliced

2 tablespoons tapioca starch

"He should have been brought straight to me! I can mend bones in a heartbeat, but growing them back. . ."

—Poppy Pomfrey,
Harry Potter and the Chamber of Secrets

1. **To make the potatoes:** Bring a large pot of salted water to a boil over medium-high heat. When the pot is boiling, add the potatoes, bring the water back to a boil, turn down the heat to medium-low, and simmer for 10 to 15 minutes or until the potatoes are very tender.

2. Drain the potatoes and return them to the pan. Put the pan back on the hot burner but with the stove off, and mash the potatoes with a potato masher until most of the steam has released. Add the cream cheese and butter and continue to mash and stir until the dairy has melted and everything is well combined. Add the salt and fresh ground pepper to taste. Set aside while making the filling.

3. **To make the filling:** Preheat the oven to 375°F.

4. In a small saucepan or microwave-safe measuring cup, heat the vegetable broth to scalding, about 1 minute in the microwave. Remove from the heat and add the cashews. Set aside.

5. Add the vegetable oil and butter to a large sauté pan over medium heat. When the butter begins to foam, add the leek and onion. Sauté until the vegetables are softened, 3 to 4 minutes, then add the mushrooms. Continue to sauté until the mixture begins to brown, another 5 to 7 minutes. Sprinkle the mixture with the tapioca starch, stir to combine, and cook for 2 more minutes, stirring slowly. Add the broth and cashews and use the liquid to deglaze the bottom of the pan. Simmer for 2 to 3 minutes until the mixture thickens slightly.

6. Pour the filling mixture into a deep pie dish or casserole pan and spread the potatoes over the top. Bake for 25 to 30 minutes or until the potatoes puff and begin to brown.

"Famous Fire Eaters"
SPICY BEEF SKEWERS

Harry Potter sneaks into Hogwarts Library's Restricted Section searching for information on Sorcerer's Stone creator Nicolas Flamel during Christmas break in *Harry Potter and the Sorcerer's Stone*. He reads aloud a few titles in the "F" section starting with *Famous Fire Eaters* before opening a book where a screaming face bulges out from the pages. The Restricted Section scenes were filmed in Oxford University's Bodleian Library, the oldest reading room at Oxford. *Famous Fire Eaters* could offer one way of grilling these extra fiery beef delights, spiced with chipotle peppers, garlic, and ginger, but it's much easier to use a grill or your oven.

> "Famous Fire Eaters. Fifteenth Century Fiends. Flamel,
> Nicolas Flamel. Where are you?"
>
> —Harry Potter,
> *Harry Potter and the Sorcerer's Stone*

Tip | If preparing as a main. as a main, the skewers can be served over rice or pasta coated in the pepper sauce.

INGREDIENTS

2 red bell peppers

1 tablespoon grapeseed or avocado oil

1 bunch cilantro leaves

1 pound flank steak, cut into thin strips about 1 inch wide

1½ teaspoons salt, divided

Juice of two limes

3 cloves black garlic, peeled

4 tablespoons whole chipotle peppers (from a can of chipotle peppers in adobo)

4 inches ginger, peeled and cut into large chunks

1 tablespoon olive oil

1 tablespoon rice vinegar

Specialty Tools
Skewers

1. Preheat the oven to 450°F.

2. Slice each pepper in half and remove the seeds and membranes. Place on a rimmed baking sheet and rub with the grapeseed oil and roast cut side down for 20 minutes or until blistered and softened. Remove from the oven and set aside until the peppers are cool enough to handle. Once they are cool, peel the skin from each pepper piece, discard, and set the peeled peppers aside.

3. Remove any wilted or bruised pieces from the cilantro bunch and rinse the rest well. Chop the stems away from the leaves, as close as you can get to the leaf top as possible. Set leaves aside.

4. In a medium well sealed container, mix the steak pieces, 1 teaspoon of salt, lime juice, 2 tablespoons of chipotle pepper that are mostly sauce, the cilantro stems, black garlic, and ginger pieces. Seal the container and shake well to coat and blend everything.

5. Refrigerate and marinate for at least 1 hour or up to 4. While the meat is marinating, make the sauce. In the bowl of a food processor, combine the roasted red bell pepper pieces, the cilantro leaves, the remaining ½ teaspoon of salt, the olive oil, and the rice vinegar. Purée in the food processor until smooth, about 1 to 2 minutes. Refrigerate until serving.

6. When ready to cook the meat, heat a grill or oven and rimmed baking sheet to 375°F. While preheating, soak 12 skewers in water for 5 minutes. When the skewers have soaked, remove them from the water and thread 1 to 2 strips of beef onto each skewer, catching it in several places, like a ribbon. Sear on each side for 1 minute and cook for 3 to 4 minutes more, turning halfway through. Serve with the sauce for dipping.

Marauder's Map
TART

To allow Harry Potter to join his classmates for a winter's trip into Hogsmeade, twins Fred and George Weasley gift him the Marauder's Map, originally created by four Hogwarts students. The map shows the location of everyone in the castle and secret passageways out of the castle leading to other places such as Honeydukes sweet shop (take the one-eyed witch passageway) or the Shrieking Shack, both in Hogsmeade. The ingredients in this savory dish evoke the Marauders—the Animagi Padfoot (Sirius Black), Prongs (James Potter), and Wormtail (Peter Pettigrew)— who protected their lycanthropic fourth member, Remus Lupin, at the full moon. The tart is topped by a Whomping Willow fashioned from the same dough as the crust, hiding the tart's hearty meat, cheese, and vegetable assortment, just as it hid an entrance into the Shrieking Shack where the Marauders met.

> **"Messrs. Moony, Wormtail, Padfoot & Prongs are proud to present the Marauder's Map."**
>
> —James Potter, Sirius Black, Remus Lupin, Peter Pettigrew, *Harry Potter and the Prisoner of Azkaban*

Continued on page 66

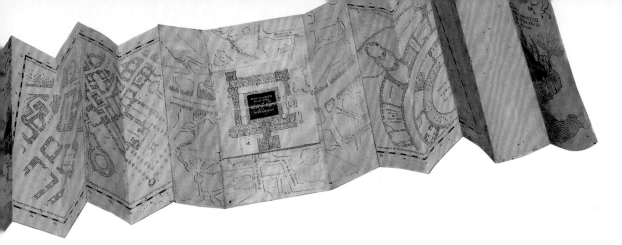

Continued from page 65

INGREDIENTS

For the Crust

2½ cups
all-purpose flour

1 teaspoon salt

½ cup unsalted butter,
very cold

¼ cup solid vegetable
shortening, very cold

About ⅓ cup ice water

1 egg

¼ teaspoon
ground nutmeg

Fresh ground pepper

For the Filling

4 ounces pancetta, diced

1 cup sliced mushrooms

2 cups baby spinach leaves,
packed

1 cup shredded
gruyere cheese

1 ounce thinly sliced
prosciutto cut
into ribbons

2 cups heavy cream

3 eggs

½ teaspoon sumac

Black pepper to taste

1. **To make the crust:** In a large bowl, combine the flour and the salt. Cut the butter and shortening into tablespoon-sized pieces and add to the flour mixture. Use a pastry cutter or 2 forks to cut into the flour. Add the water a little bit at a time and mix gently until the dough comes together.

2. Split the dough in half and roll out one half to fit a 9-inch pie dish with at least ½-inch overhang. Trim any excess dough from around the edge until you have an even ½-inch overhang, fold under and crimp as desired. Refrigerate for 30 minutes. Preheat the oven to 400°F.

3. Roll out the second half of the dough and use a pastry cutter or paring knife to cut a rough tree shape, a rounded top over a thick trunk. Transfer the dough to a baking sheet lined with a silicone baking mat or parchment paper. Cut into the rounded top creating 3 thick branches. Braid the 3 branches together once. Use the pastry cutter again to cut smaller branches from the top of each large branch. Twist and bend the branches to resemble the leafless Whomping Willow in the winter. Chill on the baking sheet for at least 30 minutes.

4. After the crust has chilled, line it with 2 pieces of overlapping aluminum foil to cover the bottom and the edges. Fill with pie weights or dried beans and bake for 10 minutes.

5. While the crust is baking, in a small bowl whisk the egg with 1 tablespoon water. Remove the crust from the oven, remove the foil and pie weights, and use a fork to prick the bottom and sides of the crust. Use a pastry brush to coat the bottom and sides of the crust with the egg wash. Return the crust to the oven and bake for another 7 to 10 minutes or until golden brown. Remove from the oven and set aside.

6. Brush the willow with the egg wash, and sprinkle with the nutmeg and a few turns of fresh ground pepper. Bake for 10 to 15 minutes or until crisp and golden brown. Remove from the oven and set aside.

7. **To make the filling:** Reduce the oven temperature to 375°F.

8. In a medium skillet over medium-high heat, add the pancetta and sauté until most of the fat has been rendered, 2 to 3 minutes. Add the mushrooms, stir to coat, and continue to cook for another 3 minutes until the mushrooms soften and begin to brown. Add spinach leaves, stir to combine, and cook until spinach is barely wilted, 1 minute.

9. Add the mixture to the bottom of the cooked pie shell. Top with the gruyere cheese and then top with prosciutto ribbons.

10. Add the cream, eggs, sumac, and pepper to a large bowl, whisking until well combined. Pour over the filling. Bake 30 to 35 minutes or until set at the edges but with a bit of jiggle in the middle.

11. Allow to cool at least 10 minutes before serving. Top with the baked Whomping Willow.

Note | The tart can be served warm, room temperature, or cold. It can be stored in an airtight container for up to 3 days.

Harry, Ron, and Hermione visit Hogsmeade, which is permanently above the snowline, in *Harry Potter and the Prisoner of Azkaban*. Concept art by Andrew Williamson.

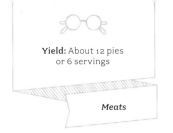
Golden Egg
MEAT PIES

For the first task of the Triwizard Tournament, Harry must capture a golden egg that, once opened, offers a clue necessary to completing the second task. Graphic designer Miraphora Mina, who devised the look of the golden egg, emphasized the idea of discovery as she planned the prop. Mina wanted Harry to break through the egg to uncover what was inside. Similarly, once your fork or fingers open these golden "eggs," you'll discover the sweetness of Italian sausage combined with tangy winter apples and fennel in a delicious triumph of tastes.

> **"Come seek us where our voices sound, we cannot sing above the ground. An hour long you'll have to look, to recover what we took."**
>
> —The Merpeople's clue for the second task,
> *Harry Potter and the Goblet of Fire*

Continued on page 72

Continued from page 71

INGREDIENTS

For the Filling

1 pound mild
Italian sausage

1 cup chopped fennel

1 medium yellow
onion, diced

1 crisp apple,
cored and diced

½ teaspoon salt

For the Crust

5 cups all-purpose flour

1 teaspoon kosher salt

2 teaspoons turmeric

1 cup vegetable
shortening, cold

1 cup unsalted
butter, cold

⅓ cup ice water

1 egg, for egg wash

Specialty Tools

Egg-shaped
cookie cutter

Other small cookie
cutters, such as leaves

1. **To make the filling:** In a large skillet over medium-high heat, brown the sausage until almost no pink is seen, about 5 minutes. Using a slotted spoon, transfer the sausage to a plate and set aside.

2. To the same skillet, add the fennel and onion, stirring to coat in the fat. Sauté for 2 to 3 minutes, stirring occasionally. Add the apple and salt, stir to combine, and continue to cook for another 3 to 5 minutes until softened and beginning to brown. Remove from the heat and mix with the sausage. Set aside to cool while making the dough.

3. **To make the crust:** In a large bowl, combine the flour, salt, and turmeric. Cut the butter and shortening into tablespoon-sized pieces and add to the flour mixture. Use a pastry cutter or 2 forks to cut into the flour. Add the water a little bit at a time and mix gently until the dough comes together.

4. **To assemble:** Line 2 baking sheets with silicone baking mats or parchment paper.

5. On a lightly floured work surface, working with ¼ of the dough at a time, roll out the dough until about ¼ inch thick. Use the cookie cutter to cut out 24 egg shapes, and reserve the scraps for decoration.

6. Lay out 6 dough eggs on each baking sheet. Top each egg with about ¼ cup filling, keeping it in the center. Cover the filling by gently stretching a second egg and placing it over the top of the filling. Use a fork to crimp the edges closed. With your fingers, gently indent the crimp edging toward the egg in spaced intervals to create a more decorative edge. When all the eggs have been assembled, roll out the scraps and use small cookie cutters to cut decorative shapes, such as leaves.

7. Mix the egg with 1 tablespoon water to create an egg wash. Brush each pie with the egg wash. Use a metal straw or a sharp knife to create a vent and add the decorations. Brush egg wash onto each decorative piece. Chill in the refrigerator while preheating the oven to 400°F. Bake for 25 to 30 minutes or until the pastry is crisp and golden brown. Allow to cool for 10 minutes before serving.

8. Store leftovers in the refrigerator for up to 4 days. The pies can be reheated in 350°F oven for 10 minutes.

Christmas Day
RACK OF LAMB

Feasts at Hogwarts are iconic scenes in the Harry Potter films, featuring flavorsome vegetable dishes such as ears of corn and mashed potatoes, brightly colored fruits, and mouthwatering entrées, among them racks of lamb dripping with juices. Another variation is the crown rack of lamb, seen at the Hogwarts Welcome Feast, called such because its circular construction topped with paper frills (called manchettes) resembles a crown. If it was served at Christmastime, it wouldn't be the only crown on the table. Set decorator Stephenie McMillan always placed Christmas crackers on the table during holiday scenes. These traditional hollow toys include a paper crown to be worn by the partygoers.

> **"Find a broomstick in your stocking,**
> **See the magic on display,**
> **Join the owls' joyous flocking,**
> **On this merry Christmas Day."**
>
> —Hogwarts Ghostly Carolers,
> *Harry Potter and the Sorcerer's Stone*

INGREDIENTS

- 8 chops or 2½ pounds rack of lamb
- 1 teaspoon salt
- Fresh ground pepper to taste
- 2 tablespoons Dijon mustard
- 2 tablespoons olive oil
- 2 teaspoons balsamic vinegar
- 1 teaspoon dried mint
- ¼ teaspoon red pepper flakes
- ¼ cup cooking sherry
- ½ cup vegetable broth, optional

1. With a rack centered in the oven preheat the oven to 425°F. Remove the lamb from the refrigerator 30 minutes before cooking. Trim the excess fat blanket by starting at the thicker side and using a sharp knife to slice the fat along the meat and away from it. Once you have a section freed you should be able to pull the rest off in one piece (a thin fat layer remaining is fine). Rub the lamb with the salt and pepper to taste. Set aside. In a small bowl, combine the mustard, olive oil, vinegar, mint, and red pepper flakes, and whisk to emulsify. Set aside.

2. Place a large ovenproof skillet over medium-high heat for 1 to 2 minutes. Place the lamb meat side down and sear until well browned, about 2 minutes. Use tongs to flip to the other side and sear for another 2 minutes. Pour off any fat drippings from the pan and discard. Use a pastry brush to cover the entire lamb rack in the mustard mixture, making sure to coat the ends.

3. Place the rack bone side down in the skillet, add the sherry to the bottom of the pan, and roast in the oven until the internal temperature of the center chop reaches 125°F for rare and 130°F for medium-rare. Remove from the oven, and tent with foil for 5 to 10 minutes before serving.

4. When ready to serve, use a carving knife to cut between the chops and serve 2 chops to each person. Serve with Quick Roasted Vegetables (page 74), Sprout's Superior Sprouts (page 45), and/or Sirius Black Hearth Potatoes (page 51).

5. If you want to make a quick pan sauce, rest the lamb on a cutting board tented with foil. Skim most of the fat from the pan and return it to the stove over medium heat. Add the vegetable broth and bring it to a simmer, deglazing the bottom of the pan. Serve each pair of chops with a spoonful of sauce.

Yield: 8 servings
Dietary Notes: GF

Meats

Christmas Eve
BEEF ROAST

A beef roast has been the most traditional of British holiday feasts since the mid-1800s, typically accompanied by potatoes and other roasted root vegetables such as Brussels sprouts (try Sprout's Superior Sprouts on page 45), and plum pudding. A boneless eye roast is one of the less expensive cuts you can use for this roast; others are beef tenderloin, ribeye, or prime rib. This succulent roast might have been served at the Christmas Eve feast for students remaining at Hogwarts over the holiday, which included the Weasley siblings and Harry Potter in *Harry Potter and the Sorcerer's Stone*. Wearing their iconic initialed sweaters, the Weasleys enjoyed Christmas Eve in the Great Hall, which was lined with pine trees decorated with crescent moons, stars, and orbs, each topped by a large gold star.

INGREDIENTS

For the Beef
One 3½ to 4½ pound boneless eye roast

1 tablespoon kosher salt

1 teaspoon black ground pepper

1 teaspoon dry thyme

1 tablespoon vegetable oil

For the Pan Gravy
½ cup red wine

1 tablespoon salted butter

1 tablespoon tapioca starch

1 cup vegetable broth

For the Quick Roasted Vegetables
4 cups mixed root vegetables such as carrot, parsnip, turnip, or bite-size new potatoes

2 tablespoons olive oil

½ teaspoon kosher salt

"**Let the feast begin!**"

—Albus Dumbledore,
Harry Potter and the Sorcerer's Stone

1. **To make the roast:** Place the meat in a shallow dish or airtight container and rub all over with the salt, black pepper, and thyme. Tightly cover with lid or plastic wrap and refrigerate for at least 4 hours or up to overnight.

2. Preheat the oven to 225°F.

3. In a large ovenproof skillet over medium-high heat, add the vegetable oil and when it begins to shimmer, add the roast. Sear the roast on all sides, 4 to 5 minutes per side. Use tongs to hold the roast steady when searing the ends and narrow sides.

4. Roast in the oven for 1 to 1½ hours, or until the meat reaches an internal temperature of 115°F.

5. Turn the oven off, leaving the roast in the oven with the door closed, for an additional 30 to 40 minutes. Remove the meat from the oven when the internal temperature reaches 125°F. Transfer the roast to a cutting board or serving platter, tent with foil, and allow to rest for 20 minutes while making the pan gravy.

6. **To make the gravy:** If making Hogwarts Yorkshire Pudding (page 55), reserve ¼ cup of drippings.

7. Add the red wine to the pan with the beef drippings over medium-high heat, and deglaze the pan, stirring and cooking the wine for 2 to 3 minutes.

8. Add the butter, stir until melted, and then sprinkle the tapioca starch over the mixture. Whisk until it forms a thick paste. Whisk in the vegetable broth and allow to simmer until thickened, 3 to 5 minutes.

9. **To make the Quick Roasted Vegetables:** While the roast is resting, preheat the oven to 375°F.

10. crub the vegetables clean and cut into uniform pieces about 2 inches in size.

11. On a large rimmed baking sheet, toss all the vegetables with the olive oil and salt and shake out to a single layer. Roast for 20 to 25 minutes or until fork tender and browning.

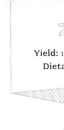

Yield: 12 to 15 servings
Dietary Notes: GF*

Fish & Fowl

Grimmauld Place
ROAST TURKEY FEAST

The Weasleys, Harry Potter, and Hermione Granger spend the Christmas holiday with Sirius Black at his home, Number Twelve, Grimmauld Place, in *Harry Potter and the Order of the Phoenix*. Molly Weasley put together a superb feast: dinner rolls, silver tureens more than likely filled with a bready stuffing and tasty vegetables, a large roast turkey with crispy brown skin, and a side of gravy on the twenty-foot-long custom-made table made by the prop makers. Turkey arrived on British shores in the 1500s and became part of the Christmas table—King Henry VIII is thought to be an early patron of this popular holiday meal.

> "Have a wondrous wizard Christmas,
> Have a merry Christmas Day.
> Move around the sparkling fire,
> Have a merry Christmas Day."
>
> —Hogwarts Ghostly Carolers,
> *Harry Potter and the Sorcerer's Stone*

Continued on page 78

Continued from page 77

INGREDIENTS

For the Brine
4 cups kosher salt

2 tablespoons peppercorns

1 tablespoon dried herbs of choice, such as sage, thyme, oregano, and/ or rosemary

12 to 15 pound fresh turkey, giblets and neck removed

For the Stuffing
15 cups (about 1½ pounds) lightly packed bread cubes (see note)

12 ounces mushrooms of preference

1 yellow onion

1 bunch celery, outer stalks removed

1 pound bulk sausage

2 tablespoons unsalted butter, plus more for greasing

4 to 6 cups low sodium vegetable broth

2 tablespoons salted butter, optional

For Roasting the Turkey
6 tablespoons unsalted butter

Turkey lacing kit

Specialty Tools
Brining bag or large pot big enough to hold the turkey and space in the refrigerator or a large cooler filled with ice

Large roasting pan with a V-rack

1. **To make the brine:** Fill a large pot with 1 gallon water and add the salt, peppercorns, and desired herb combination.

2. Heat over medium-high heat, stirring until all the salt is dissolved. Remove from the heat and add 1 gallon ice water. Stir until the ice melts and refrigerate the mixture until it is completely cool.

3. If using a brining bag, place the turkey breast side down in the bag and rest in a roasting pan for support. Fill the bag with the cooled brine mixture and seal well. Place in the refrigerator or cooler and brine for at least 30 minutes per pound, or up to 1 hour per pound. If using a pot, place the turkey neck end down and pour in the brine, cover, and proceed as above.

4. **To make the stuffing:** Preheat the oven to 250°F and spread the bread cubes out in single layers on 2 rimmed baking sheets (you may need to work in batches to toast all the bread). Let the bread toast in the oven for 20 minutes, then turn the oven off and allow to cool. This can be done up to 3 days ahead. Store the bread in an airtight container or plastic bag.

5. Thinly slice the mushrooms and set aside. Dice the onion and the celery, using the whole heart and leaves, and set aside, keeping separate from the mushrooms.

6. In a large skillet over medium-high heat, add the sausage to the pan and brown, 5 to 7 minutes, breaking up into small pieces with a wooden spoon. When the sausage is brown, use slotted spoon to remove the meat to a plate and set aside.

7. Add the butter to the same skillet and when it begins to foam, add the mushrooms. Sauté the mushrooms, stirring occasionally until they are starting to brown, 2 to 3 minutes. Add the onion and celery and continue to cook, stirring to combine, until the celery and onion are softened, another 3 to 5 minutes. Remove from the heat and transfer to a very large bowl, add the sausage to the vegetable mixture, and stir to combine.

8. Add the bread cubes and stir to combine. Start to add the vegetable broth, 1 cup at a time, until the mixture is well moistened and starts to hold together. Transfer about a third of the stuffing to a greased casserole dish.

9. If stuffing the turkey, continue to add broth to the remaining stuffing until it is quite wet but still holds together. Use the wetter stuffing to stuff the cavities of the turkey.

10. Press the stuffing into an even layer in the casserole dish, cover with foil, and refrigerate until needed. To heat and serve, preheat the oven to 350°F and bake, covered, for 30 minutes. Uncover, dot with the salted butter, if desired, and continue to bake until the center temperature reads 165°F.

11. **To roast the turkey:** Place the oven rack to lowest position and preheat the oven to 325°F.

12. Remove the turkey from the brine, rinse it and pat it dry with paper towels. If stuffing the bird, loosely fill the cavities with stuffing and truss closed. Using a pastry brush, brush the turkey skin all over with the melted butter. Add 1 cup of water to the bottom of the pan.

13. Place the turkey breast side down on the roasting rack in the roasting pan. Roast breast side down for 2 hours, basting once with the pan drippings.

14. After 2 hours, remove the turkey from the oven and using silicone oven mitts or thick stacks of paper towel for each hand, grab the turkey at both ends and turn it breast side up. Baste with more pan drippings and return to the oven. Roast for another 1 to 1½ hours or until the thigh temperature reaches 175°F and, if used, the stuffing in the center of the bird reaches 165°F.

15. Remove the turkey from the oven, tent with foil, and let rest for 20 minutes before carving. Serve with stuffing, Quick Roasted Vegetables (page 74), Sprout's Superior Sprouts (page 45), and/or Sirius Black Hearth Potatoes (page 51).

Note | For the bread cubes you can use a variety of breads and it is wonderful to mix them. Sourdough, black bread, multigrain, or even loaves with nuts and dried fruit can add fantastic texture to the stuffing.

To make this recipe gluten-free, you can use store-bought gluten-free stuffing mix or substitute gluten-free bread cubes.

Yield: 2 servings as an entrée
or 6 as an appetizer
Dietary Notes: GF

Fish & Fowl

Beauxbatons
FRENCH FISH

Perhaps the women of Beauxbatons Academy of Magic would have enjoyed having this French-inspired oyster-based entrée served at the Yule Ball; it would certainly match the other shellfish on the menu. With a classic combination of French flavors such as apple, fennel, and shallots, this stands out like the French blue of the Beauxbatons students' outfits. This dish can be served either cold and raw, or cooked and hot. Fleur Delacour and her classmates might have preferred the warmer version, as costume designer Jany Temime purposely chose a light silk fabric for their costumes, wanting them to appear inappropriately dressed for Hogwarts' cool Scottish weather.

> "The champion from Beauxbatons Academy—
> Fleur Delacour!"
>
> —Albus Dumbledore,
> *Harry Potter and the Goblet of Fire*

INGREDIENTS

4 tablespoons white balsamic vinegar

½ teaspoon salt, plus more for the oysters

½ teaspoon sugar

½ green apple, peeled, cored, and diced

2 tablespoons finely minced shallot

1 tablespoon finely minced fennel, with fronds if possible

12 small fresh oysters

1. In a small bowl, combine the vinegar, salt, and sugar, and stir to dissolve. Add in the apple, shallot, and fennel, and stir again. Allow to sit at room temperature for 30 minutes to let the flavors meld. If not using after 30 minutes, store in an airtight container in the refrigerator for up to 3 days.

2. When ready to serve, scrub the oysters and discard any that remain open. Shuck the oysters and place them on an oyster platter or regular serving dish with a bed of salt. Place about 1 teaspoon of sauce on each oyster and have the rest available in a small dish with a spoon.

3. **If you're not a fan of raw oysters, here is a cooked version:** Preheat the oven to 300°F.

4. Scrub the oysters, discarding any that remain open, and place them on a rimmed baking sheet.

5. Bake for 3 to 5 minutes until they just pop open.

6. While they are baking, add 2 tablespoons unsalted butter to a small sauté pan over medium heat. When the butter begins to foam, add the apple-vinegar mixture and sauté until most of the liquid has absorbed, 2 to 3 minutes. Remove from heat and set aside.

7. Remove the oysters from the oven and set the oven to high broil. Open each oyster and free the meat from its shell, nestling it back inside. Top each oyster with about 2 teaspoons apple mixture and broil 2 to 3 minutes or until the apple mixture begins to brown. Serve immediately.

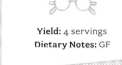
Yule Ball
ENGLISH FISH PIE

The classic English Fish Pie dates back to the 1600s, and became a piscatory alternative to Shepherd's Pie, named "Fisherman's Pie" as it substituted fish for lamb under its creamy mashed potato crust. Seafood was served at the Yule Ball in *Harry Potter and the Goblet of Fire*, though as a cold dish, not a hearty hot one. The set decoration team went to London's famous fish market, Billingsgate, for their entrée. You needn't go so far, as this dish is all about doing things easily.

INGREDIENTS

For the Mashed Potatoes

1½ pounds gold potatoes, cubed

2 tablespoons unsalted butter

½ cup grated Parmesan cheese, divided

Salt and freshly ground pepper, to taste

For the Pie Filling

1 tablespoon olive oil

1 tablespoon salted butter

2 carrots, diced

4 green onions, white and light green parts, thinly sliced

2 cloves garlic, diced

½ cup heavy cream

1 pound cod, haddock, or white sea bass

½ cup parsley leaves, packed, roughly chopped

Juice and zest of one lemon

½ teaspoon salt

"Blimey, Harry, you slay dragons. If you can't get a date, who can?"

"I think I'll take the dragon right now."

—Ron Weasley and Harry Potter, *Harry Potter and the Goblet of Fire*

1. **To make the potatoes:** Bring a large pot of salted water to a boil over medium heat. Add the cubed potatoes. Bring back to a boil and simmer, over medium heat, for 10 to 15 minutes or until the potatoes are very tender.

2. Drain the potatoes and return them to the hot pot. Place the pot on the stove, and with the burner off, mash the potatoes gently until most of the steam has been released. Add the butter and ¼ cup Parmesan cheese and stir until the butter is melted. Continue to stir briskly until the potatoes are light and fluffy. Taste, and adjust seasoning with fresh ground pepper and salt. Set aside until needed.

3. **To make the filling:** Preheat the oven 375°F.

4. In a medium skillet over medium-high heat, add the olive oil and butter. When the butter begins to foam, add the carrots, green onions, and garlic. Sauté until the vegetables are tender, about 3 minutes.

5. Add the cream and continue cooking and stirring until the cream reduces and thickens, 3 to 5 minutes. Pour into a 9-inch-by-9-inch casserole dish and set aside.

6. Cut the fish into 1-inch chunks, looking carefully for and removing any pin bones. In a medium bowl, mix the fish with the parsley, lemon zest, lemon juice, and salt. Scatter the fish mixture over the vegetable mixture in the casserole dish.

7. Using a soup spoon, scoop the mashed potatoes on top of the fish in big dollops, covering the surface. Gently spread each dollop with the back of the spoon to create a scale pattern. Sprinkle the remaining ¼ cup parmesan cheese over the top. Bake for 20 to 25 minutes, or until brown and bubbly. Leftovers can be stored in an airtight container for 24 hours.

DESSERTS

KEEP

APPL...

BALL...

GAE...

CHU...

FAL...

HO...

...PIES

...D

...RS

...BATS

...y CATAPULTS

...Y CANNONS

FALMOUTH FALCONS

HOLYHEAD HARPIES

KENMARE KESTRELS

MONTROSE MAGPIES

PRIDE OF PORTREE

PUDDLEMERE UNITED

TUTSHILL TORNADOS

WIGTOWN WANDERERS

WIMBOURNE WASPS

TOTAL

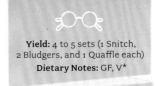

Yield: 4 to 5 sets (1 Snitch,
2 Bludgers, and 1 Quaffle each)
Dietary Notes: GF, V*

Giftable Treats

Golden Snitch
POPCORN BALLS

Harry Potter becomes the youngest Seeker in a
century at Hogwarts when he's recruited to play for
the Gryffindor Quidditch team in *Harry Potter and the
Sorcerer's Stone*. A Seeker's responsibility is to catch
the Golden Snitch, a small ball that darts around like
a hummingbird worth 150 points when caught, ending
the game. Several designs were considered for the
Golden Snitch's wings to give it credible aerodynamics
but the wings on these won't need to fly far—only into
your mouth as a sweet holiday treat. Other balls in the
game are Bludgers, hit by Beaters to distract players,
and the Quaffle ball, which scores points when thrown
through a hoop, also represented in this recipe.

> "The only ball I want you to worry
> about is this . . . the Golden Snitch."
>
> —Oliver Wood,
> *Harry Potter and the Sorcerer's Stone*

INGREDIENTS

20 cups popped popcorn
(about ¾ cup of kernels)

1 tablespoon water

1 cup golden syrup

1 cup mini marshmallows

2 cups powdered sugar

½ teaspoon salt

¼ cup unsalted butter, plus
more for greasing hands

½ cup gold sanding sugar

2 tablespoons
black cocoa powder

¼ cup cocoa powder

1 cup white chocolate chips,
optional

10 wooden toothpicks, optional

Gold luster dust, optional

Continued on page 88

Continued from page 87

1. Line 2 baking sheets with silicone baking mats or parchment paper. Have extra softened butter standing by for greasing hands. Place the popped popcorn in a very large bowl.

2. Add the water, golden syrup, marshmallows, powdered sugar, salt, and butter to a medium saucepan. Bring to a boil over medium heat, stirring continuously, until all the marshmallows are melted and mixture is smooth.

3. Remove from the heat and pour over the popcorn, stirring quickly to combine. Make sure to incorporate all the syrup mixture, scraping it off the bottom of the bowl. Allow to sit for 1 to 2 minutes.

4. Using buttered hands, create the snitches by using about 2 tablespoons of the popcorn mixture and shaping it into a tight ball. Place on one of the baking sheets. Next create pairs of bludgers, by using about ½ cup of the mixture, shape into tight balls of equal size and place on a baking sheet. You will need to regrease your hands periodically.

5. To create the quaffles, use about 1½ cups of the mixture. Form tight balls, as above, but once formed hold the ball in your two hands and use your thumbs and pointer fingers to create the signature indentations. Make three deep dents in the "sides" of the ball and 2 shallow indents, 1 on the top and 1 on the bottom. Place on the baking sheets.

6. **To decorate:** Pour the sanding sugar into a shallow bowl and roll each snitch in the sugar to coat completely. Set aside (extra sugar can be reused).

7. Place the black cocoa powder into a separate shallow bowl and working above the bowl use a pastry brush to dust the entire surface of each bludger. Repeat with a clean bowl, the cocoa powder, and the quaffles.

8. **To make the wings for the snitches:** In a microwave-safe bowl, melt the white chocolate in 30 second bursts for a total of 1 minute. Stir until smooth. Lay a piece of parchment paper on a flat work surface. Using a narrow carving knife, coat the top 3 inches of the knife on one side in a thick layer of chocolate. Press the tip of the knife against the parchment and draw the knife toward you smearing the chocolate like you would paint on a palette, creating a feather shape. Place a toothpick in the center of the feather leaving about ½ inch exposed. If needed, spread a bit more chocolate over the toothpick to cover. Use the tines of a fork to gently scrape the "feathers" into the chocolate, working from one side to the other, being careful not to go all the way through. Repeat the process, making sure to pull the fork the opposite direction to create a mirrored wing. Continue until you have enough sets of wings. Leave the wings to set for 5 minutes.

9. Once the wings are set, carefully remove them from the parchment and hold with the toothpick. Gently brush both sides with gold luster dust. Insert the wings into the snitch popcorn balls just before serving, using the exposed toothpick end.

Note | The chocolate wings are very fragile so you will want to make extra sets. If a sturdier set of wings is desired there are many premade paper ones available online. Just make sure to inform guests the wings are décor only and not edible. This can be made vegetarian by using vegetarian marshmallows.

Hagrid's
PUMPKIN SEED BRITTLE

It's not just the flesh inside a pumpkin that can be used to make sweet or savory dishes—pumpkin seeds can be used for any number of snacks and desserts, and it wouldn't be surprising for someone like Hagrid to utilize every part of the pumpkins he grows in his garden. Though peanut brittle is a Southern American confection, it has been adapted around the world, and this pumpkin seed version is highly nutritious—and delicious.

> **"I've got presents?"**
>
> —Harry Potter,
> *Harry Potter and the Sorcerer's Stone*

INGREDIENTS

1½ cups sugar

½ cup corn syrup

½ cup plus 2 tablespoons water

2 cups roasted salted pumpkin seeds

1 tablespoon unsalted butter, plus more for greasing

1 teaspoon baking soda

1 teaspoon vanilla

2 teaspoons coarse finishing salt

1. Grease a rimmed baking sheet with butter.

2. Place the sugar, corn syrup, water, and pumpkin seeds in a 2-quart microwave-safe bowl. Cook on high/maximum power for 7 minutes. Carefully remove from the microwave with pot holders, place on a heatproof surface, and gently stir to combine.

3. Cook again on high/maximum power for 15 to 17 minutes or until syrup separates into threads. This is the hard-crack candy stage or 300°F on a candy thermometer. While this is cooking, measure out the butter, baking soda, and vanilla into separate small bowls, and have standing by.

4. Once nuts and syrup reach the hard-crack stage, carefully remove from the microwave, as above, and stir in the butter, baking soda, and vanilla just until light in color and bubbly.

5. Pour onto the buttered baking sheet on a heatproof surface, and spread in a thin layer. Sprinkle finishing salt across the entire surface while warm. Allow to cool completely and break into pieces. Store in an airtight container at room temperature for up to one week.

Every Flavor
CAKE POPS

At their first Christmas together, in *Harry Potter and the Sorcerer's Stone*, Ron munches on a box of Bertie Bott's Every-Flavour Beans while he watches Harry open his presents. These cake pops evoke this popular wizarding candy, imitating its red, white, and yellow packaging, which was created by graphic artists Miraphora Mina and Eduardo Lima. Every cake pop has a bean on top. Consumers will have to guess which pop to dare to have, for not all the beans are sweet—the candy also features other flavors such as earwax or bogies. Will the inside have a matching flavorful yummy bean or the opposite?

> **"They mean every flavor. There's chocolate and peppermint, and there's also spinach, liver, and tripe."**
>
> —Ron Weasley,
> *Harry Potter and the Sorcerer's Stone*

Continued on page 92

Continued from page 91

INGREDIENTS

3 cups cake crumbs (about half Triwizard Trifle cake recipe (page 131)

2 ounces cream cheese, softened

2 tablespoons butter, softened

¼ cup white chocolate chips, melted

3 ouncesnBertie Bott's Every Flavour Beans

20 ounces white melting chocolate, divided

5 ounces red candy melts

5 ounces yellow candy melts

Specialty Tools

16 lollipop sticks

2 small, clean craft brushes

1. In a large bowl, combine the cake crumbs, cream cheese, and butter. Use a hand mixer fitted with paddle attachments on low to mix until a dough starts to come together. Scrape down the sides of the bowl and add the melted chocolate. Mix again on medium until all the ingredients are homogenous and the dough begins to pull away from the sides of the bowl.

2. Line a baking sheet with a silicone baking mat or parchment paper. Sort out the beans: decide how many "surprise" cake pops you will have. Match flavors together creating 16 pairs. For the surprise pops, create pairs with similar colors, such as Green Apple and Grass or Marshmallow and Earwax.

3. In a microwave-safe bowl, melt about 1 ounce of the white melting chocolate for 30 seconds, and stir until smooth.

4. Using about 2 tablespoons of the cake mixture, form a cake pop, and place it on the lined baking sheet. Repeat with the remaining cake mixture. Dip the end of each lollipop stick in the melted chocolate and then push the stick into each cake pop, at least 1 inch. Press a bean into the side of each pop making sure it is well secured but still visible. Set the matching/paired beans aside. Freeze the cake pops for 1 hour.

5. Toward the end of the freezing time, melt the remaining white chocolate in a melting pot or a microwave-safe bowl in 30 second bursts. Stir until smooth.

6. Working with 1 cake pop at a time, note the bean inserted into the cake, find its mate, and then dip the pop in the chocolate. Make sure to cover the whole pop, up to the stick, shake off excess chocolate, and place back on the baking sheet. Immediately press the matching bean into the chocolate. Repeat with the remaining cake pops.

7. Leave the cake pops to set for 5 to 10 minutes.

8. Add the candy melts to 2 separate small bowls, and microwave in 30 second bursts for 1 minute. Stir until smooth. Use small, clean craft brushes to paint red and yellow stripes on the cake pops. Allow to set another 5 minutes.

9. Once set, the cake pops can be stored in an airtight container in a cool dry place for up to 3 days. Or wrap in cellophane bags as gifts.

Ginny's Mini Mincemeat
TARTS

Mincemeat pies, in any size, are integral to a British Christmas. And while they did start out in the Middle Ages with minced mutton or beef, they shifted to the fruit and candied peel version in Victorian times. English tradition maintains that when combining the mincemeat ingredients, one should stir in a clockwise direction and make a wish. In *Harry Potter and the Half-Blood Prince*, Ginny feeds Harry a tiny tart like these during the holiday at the Weasleys', and that turned out very well.

> **"Open up, you."**
>
> —Ginny Weasley to Harry Potter,
> *Harry Potter and the Half-Blood Prince*

Continued on page 96

Continued from page 95

INGREDIENTS

For the Mincemeat
1 lemon, for zest and juice

2 crisp apples, peeled, cored, and chopped

2 teaspoons unsalted butter

1 cup dark brown sugar, firmly packed

¼ cup apple juice

1 cup golden raisins

1 cup currants

1 ounce candied ginger, diced

2 teaspoons orange marmalade

¼ teaspoon ground clove

For the Pastry
2½ cups all-purpose flour

1 teaspoon salt

2 teaspoons powdered sugar

½ teaspoon cinnamon

½ cup unsalted butter, very cold

¼ cup solid vegetable shortening, very cold

⅓ cup ice water

Specialty Tools
12 capacity muffin tin

3½-inch round cookie cutter or pastry wheel

A 2-inch star or round cookie cutter

1. **To make the mincemeat:** Zest the lemon and set the zest aside in a small bowl. In a medium saucepan, combine the apples, butter, and the juice of the lemon, and cook over medium heat until the apples soften, about 5 minutes. Add the brown sugar and the apple juice and continue to cook until all the sugar is dissolved, another 5 to 7 minutes.

2. Add the raisins, currants, ginger, marmalade, and clove, and stir until well combined. Continue to cook until the mixture thickens enough to coat the back of a spoon, about 10 minutes. Transfer to a bowl and allow to cool completely before filling the tart shells.

3. **To make the pastry:** In a large bowl, combine the flour, salt, powdered sugar, and cinnamon. Cut the butter and shortening into tablespoon-size pieces and add to the flour mixture. Use a pastry cutter or 2 forks to cut into the flour. Add the ice water a little bit at a time and mix gently until the dough comes together.

4. Grease the cavities of the muffin tin well with butter. Roll out half the pastry dough to about ⅛ inch thick. Use the cookie cutter to cut out 3½-inch circles and press gently into the bottom of each muffin tin cavity. Keep the sides as straight as possible and make sure the dough goes all the way to the bottom of the tin. Use the tines of a fork to crimp the edges of each tart shell. Refrigerate the tin with the tart shells.

5. Roll out the second half of dough and cut out 2-inch stars or rounds, transfer to a baking sheet and refrigerate for at least 15 minutes. Preheat the oven to 375°F.

6. Fill each cavity with about 3 tablespoons filling, top with a pastry star or circle, and bake for 20 to 25 minutes until the filling is bubbly and the pastry is golden brown. Allow to cool in the pan for 15 minutes before using an offset spatula to remove them from the tin. Allow to cool completely on a wire rack before storing in an airtight container between layers of parchment paper. These can be kept at room temperature for up to 3 days.

A starry winter night outside the Burrow, the home of the Weasley family, in concept art by Andrew Williamson for *Harry Potter and the Half-Blood Prince*.

Yield: Three 6-inch cakes
Dietary Notes: V

Great Hall Holiday
FRUITCAKE

The British fruitcake—also known as a Christmas cake—
is packed with seasonal dried fruits such as cherries and
apricots that give it sweetness and slivered almonds
that add a tasty texture. Fruit and nut cakes became
extremely popular in the British Isles during the Middle
Ages. It's not surprising, then, that this would be served at
a feast at Hogwarts as the school was founded in the
middle of the Middle Ages. A touch of brandy will make
eating this as cozy as sitting at one of the 100-foot-long
Great Hall house tables in front of the massive fireplace.

> **"Ding dong, ding dong,**
> **Ring the Hogwarts bell!"**
>
> —Hogwarts Ghostly Carolers,
> *Harry Potter and the Sorcerer's Stone*

Continued on page 100

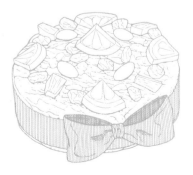

Continued from page 99

INGREDIENTS

½ cup golden raisins

½ cup dried cherries, diced

1 cup dried apricot halves, diced

1½ cups brandy, divided

1 cup salted butter, plus more for greasing

1½ cups dark brown sugar, firmly packed

½ cup granulated sugar

4 eggs, separated

2 cups slivered almonds

2½ cups all-purpose flour, divided, plus more for the pans

1 teaspoon baking powder

½ teaspoon salt

½ teaspoon nutmeg

½ teaspoon allspice

Specialty Tools

Three 6-inch cake pans

Three 15-by-15-inch pieces of cheesecloth

Three 15-by-15-inch pieces of foil

1. In a large container with a tight-fitting lid, combine the raisins, cherries, and apricots. Cover with the brandy, stir to combine, cover, and let soak overnight at room temperature.

2. Drain the fruit over a bowl, reserving the fruit and the liquid.

3. Grease the cake pans with butter, line the bottoms with rounds of parchment paper, and flour the sides. Preheat the oven to 275°F.

4. In the bowl of a stand mixer, beat the butter until light and fluffy, about 1 minute. Add the brown sugar and granulated sugar a little at a time. Continue mixing until well blended.

5. Add the egg yolks, one at a time, mixing after each addition and scraping down the sides of the bowl.

6. In a medium bowl, combine the almonds with ½ cup flour, and set aside. In another medium bowl combine the remaining 2 cups flour with the baking powder, salt, nutmeg, and allspice.

7. Add half the flour mixture to the butter mixture and mix until well combined. Add the reserved fruit liquid and mix again, scraping down the sides of the bowl. Add the remaining flour and mix until well combined. Set aside.

8. In another bowl, using the stand mixer or a hand mixer, beat the egg whites until stiff peaks form. Fold the egg whites into the batter, followed by the fruit and then the nuts. Split the batter evenly between the three pans, approximately 2 cups each. Bake for 1 to 1½ hours or until a cake tester comes out clean and the cake is golden brown. Allow to cool in the pan for 15 minutes before using an offset spatula to gently separate the edges of the cake from the pan and inverting onto a cooling rack. Flip again and cool right side up.

9. When the cakes are completely cool, soak the pieces of cheesecloth in the remaining ½ cup brandy. Lay down a piece of foil, cover it with a piece of soaked cheesecloth and place a cake in the center. Wrap the cake, first in the cheesecloth and then in the foil. Repeat with the remaining cakes.

10. Store the cakes in the refrigerator for up to 3 months. The cakes can be eaten immediately but are best made at least a month ahead to let the flavors develop and the brandy soak in. If making a month or more ahead, check the cakes every two weeks, and if the cheese cloth is dry, spritz with more brandy and rewrap.

11. When serving, the fruitcake can be decorated with dried fruits and nuts and even tied with a ribbon.

Harry's Favorite
TREACLE TART

Treacle tart is a quintessential British teatime—or anytime—dessert and known to be a favorite of Harry Potter. Treacle is a byproduct of the sugar-making process and comes in both light and dark varieties. This recipe uses golden syrup, the lighter form of treacle, combined with lemon and breadcrumbs to make a custard-like filling that has the added sweetness of chocolate chips.

> "Happy Christmas, Harry."
>
> "Happy Christmas, Ron."
>
> —Ron Weasley and Harry Potter,
> *Harry Potter and the Sorcerer's Stone*

INGREDIENTS

½ recipe pastry from Wizard Chess Pie (page 107), but substitute ½ teaspoon of ginger for cinnamon

Zest and juice of 1 lemon

1 cup golden syrup

2 eggs

1½ cups fresh white breadcrumbs

½ cup semi-sweet chocolate chips

Whipped cream, for serving (optional)

Specialty Tools
9-inch loose bottom tart tin or ceramic tart tin

1. On a lightly floured surface, roll out the dough and fit it to your tart pan. If using a loose bottom tin, trim the dough with the edge of the tin by pressing the overhang against the edge. If using a ceramic pan, use a sharp knife to trim the edge. Refrigerate for 30 minutes.

2. Toward the end of the refrigeration, preheat the oven to 425°F.

3. Once chilled, line the tart shell with foil and fill with pie weights or dried beans. Bake for 10 minutes.

4. Remove from the oven, remove the foil and weights, and prick all over the bottom and side with a fork. Return to the oven for 10 minutes.

5. While the crust is baking, prepare the filling by adding to a large bowl the lemon juice and zest, golden syrup, and eggs. Whisk together until well blended. Add the breadcrumbs and fold in until well combined.

6. Remove the tart shell from the oven and scatter the chocolate chips on the bottom. Let stand for 5 minutes.

7. Pour in the filling, level it out, and bake for 20 to 25 minutes until golden brown and set, but still with a bit of jiggle in the middle. Allow to cool on a wire rack. The tart can be served warm or cold. Serve with whipped cream if desired.

SNOWY BURROW CAKE

Harry spends Christmas at The Burrow in *Harry Potter and the Half-Blood Prince*, where the holiday table is set with golden Christmas crackers, mismatched china, and a cake topped with tall, tree-shaped peaks of white frosting (and a figure-skating snowman). This sponge cake, iconically British, swaps in snowmen-shaped truffles for a topper. The Weasley home is quirky, playful, and warm. Set designer Stephenie McMillan wanted the house to appear that most everything in it was bought in second-hand shops, acquired at swap meets, or rescued from curbs.The house itself was made to seem as if Arthur Weasley built it all.

> "Ding dong, ding dong,
>
> Make the Christmas morning bright.
>
> Fly high across the sky,
>
> Light the Christmas night."
>
> —Hogwarts Ghostly Carolers, *Harry Potter and the Sorcerer's Stone*

INGREDIENTS

For the Cake Batter
3 eggs

1 cup whole milk

Zest of 1 small orange

2 tablespoons fresh orange juice

1 teaspoon vanilla paste or vanilla extract

2¼ cups all-purpose flour

1¼ cups sugar

4 teaspoons baking powder

¼ teaspoon salt

¾ cup (1½ sticks) salted butter, softened

For the Truffles
6 ounces white chocolate

¼ cup heavy whipping cream

¼ teaspoon orange extract

¼ teaspoon ground ginger

Cornstarch for dusting hands

6 ounces white candy melts or additional white chocolate (see note)

Gumdrop, licorice, and nonpareils, optional

For the Frosting and Filling
12 ounces white chocolate

18 ounces cream cheese, softened

1¼ cups unsalted butter, softened

2 tablespoons orange juice

1 teaspoon vanilla

¼ cup orange marmalade

4 to 6 pretzel sticks, optional

Large open star tip, optional

Opal sparkle sugar, optional

Specialty Tools
Two 8-inch cake pans

Continued on page 104

Continued from page 103

1. **To make the cake batter:** Line the bottom of both cake pans with rounds of parchment paper. Preheat the oven to 350°F.

2. Whisk the eggs in a medium bowl. Add the milk, orange zest, orange juice, and vanilla, whisk to combine. Set aside.

3. In the bowl of a stand mixer fitted with the paddle attachment (or in a large mixing bowl using a hand mixer), combine the flour, sugar, baking powder, and salt. Stir until combined. Add the softened butter, stirring on low until a coarse crumb mixture forms.

4. Reserve ½ cup of the egg mixture and add the rest to the batter mixture. Mix on medium (or high if using a hand mixer) for about 2 minutes. Stop the mixer. Add the remaining ½ cup egg mixture, and beat for 1 minute more. Stop the mixer again, scrape down the sides of the bowl, and mix about 30 seconds more. Split the batter between the cake pans and bake for 20 to 25 minutes or until a cake tester comes out clean. Allow to cool in the pan for 15 minutes, then use an offset spatula to loosen the edge and invert onto a wire cooling rack.

5. **To make the truffles:** Place the chocolate in a microwave-safe bowl and pour the heavy whipping cream over it. Heat in the microwave for 1 minute, allow to stand for 5 minutes, and stir until smooth. Stir in the orange extract and ginger. Cover and refrigerate for 2 to 3 hours or until firm enough to work with.

6. Have a baking sheet lined with a silicone mat or parchment ready. Remove the chocolate mixture from the refrigerator. Dust your hands with a bit of cornstarch and make 4 large balls, about 2 tablespoons each, by rolling the mixture in your hands. Make an additional 4 small balls, about 2 teaspoons each. Leave the truffles on the tray while you melt the coating.

7. Melt the coating of choice (see note) in a microwave-safe bowl, then stir until smooth.

8. Dip each ball into the coating, shake off the excess and return it to the baking sheet. Save any extra coating to attach décor.

9. When all the truffles have been coated, place the baking sheet in the refrigerator for 5 minutes to set. To make the snowman, use a bit of coating to glue one large and one small truffle together.

10. Decorate with a gumdrop hat, licorice scarf, and nonpareil eyes and buttons, using more coating to attach. Store the snowman and the remaining truffles, in an airtight container, in the refrigerator until serving.

11. **To make the frosting:** In a microwave-safe bowl, melt the chocolate in 30-second bursts, stirring between each one. Stir until completely smooth.

12. In the bowl of a stand mixer fitted with a paddle attachment, beat the cream cheese until smooth and fluffy, about 2 minutes. Scrape down the sides of the bowl. Add the chocolate in 3 batches, beating on low for 30 seconds and then high for 30 seconds more after each addition. Once all the chocolate is added, scrape down the bowl again. With the mixer running on medium-low, begin adding the butter, 1 tablespoon at a time, until it is all incorporated. Scrape the bowl again, switch to a whisk attachment, and add the orange juice and vanilla. Whip on high for 30 seconds to 1 minute, until light and fluffy.

13. Mix 1 cup of frosting with the marmalade and set aside.

14. **To assemble the cake:** Smear a bit of frosting on a cake plate or cake board and place the bottom layer on it. Frost the top of the bottom layer with the marmalade frosting mixture, spreading it evenly out to the sides. Top this with the second layer and use the remaining frosting to frost the entire cake, top and sides. To add the trees, fit a pastry bag with a large open star tip and fill with the remaining frosting. Wherever you want a tree, pipe a large "star" mound to create the base. Insert a pretzel stick into the center of this base and insert the star tip over it, pushing gently to the base of the pretzel stick. Continue to pipe stars as you move the bag up the stick. Make sure to use less pressure with each star, creating smaller ones as you go. Refrigerate until an hour before serving.

15. When you remove the cake from the refrigerator, you can decorate with the snowman and extra "snowballs." Use the sparkle sugar to create the snowman's skate lines.

Note | White chocolate is off-white. For a snowier look coat the truffles with the white candy melt coating.

Sleepy
CUPCAKES

During the Christmas holiday in *Harry Potter and the Chamber of Secrets*, Harry, Ron, and Hermione endeavor to find the Heir of Slytherin, a descendant of Salazar Slytherin who has released the murderous Basilisk within the Chamber of Secrets to attack Muggle-born students. To do so, Hermione brews Polyjuice Potion so Harry and Ron can enter the Slytherin dormitory disguised as Draco Malfoy's cronies, Crabbe and Goyle. Their task is almost too easy as the Slytherins grab two floating cupcakes filled with a sleeping draught. These fluffy cupcakes will seem light enough to float themselves, with their tangy orange flavor and chocolate ganache topping.

> **"I've filled these with a simple sleeping draught. Simple but powerful."**
>
> —Hermione Granger,
> *Harry Potter and the Chamber of Secrets*

INGREDIENTS

For the Cake
3 eggs
1 cup whole milk
1 tablespoon vanilla extract
Zest from 1 orange
1 tablespoon orange juice
2¼ cups all-purpose flour
1¼ cups sugar
4 teaspoons baking powder
1 half teaspoon kosher salt

¾ cups unsalted butter, softened

For the Ganache
1 cup semisweet chocolate chips
1 cup cream
2 tablespoons orange sprinkles

Specialty Tools
Two 12-cup capacity muffin tins

1. **To make the cake:** Preheat oven to 350°F. Line the two 12-cup capacity muffin tins with liners.

2. Whisk the eggs in a medium bowl. Add the milk, vanilla, orange juice, and zest. Whisk until combined and set aside.

3. In the bowl of a stand mixer fitted with the paddle attachment (or in a large mixing bowl using a hand mixer), combine the flour, sugar, baking powder, and salt. Mix until combined. Add the softened butter, stirring on low until a coarse crumb mixture forms.

4. Reserving ½ cup of the milk mixture, add the rest to the flour mixture. Mix on medium (or high if using a hand mixer) for about 2 minutes. Stop the mixer, add the remaining ½ cup milk, and beat for 1 minute more.

5. Stop the mixer again, scrape down the sides of the bowl, and mix about 30 seconds more. Fill each muffin liner half full. Bake for 15 to 20 minutes or until a cake tester comes out clean. Allow the cupcakes to cool in the pan on a wire rack before removing. Allow to cool completely before frosting.

6. **To make the ganache:** Add the chocolate chips to a medium microwave-safe bowl and pour the cream over them. Heat in the microwave for 1 minute and then allow to stand for 5 minutes. Stir until smooth. Allow to cool about 10 minutes or until spreadable.

7. Spread a dollop of ganache onto the center of each cupcake and top with sprinkles.

8. Cupcakes can be stored in a cool place in an airtight container for up to 3 days.

WIZARD CHESS PIE

While endeavoring to find the Sorcerer's Stone, Harry, Ron, and Hermione must pass through a series of security obstacles including a three-headed dog, flying keys, and a deadly game of wizard chess. Ron is a talented player of the game and guides his friends to a win that allows Harry to continue on to locate the stone. The "marble" of the chessboard's squares was created by squirting oil paint into a six-foot square tank of water and then placing paper on top to absorb the swirling colors. This pie needs only a few drops of food coloring to create the board's black squares.

> **"That's wizard chess!"**
>
> —Ron Weasley,
> *Harry Potter and the Sorcerer's Stone*

INGREDIENTS

For the Pastry

2½ cups all-purpose flour

2 tablespoons sugar, divided

1 teaspoon salt

2 teaspoons ground cinnamon, divided

½ cup unsalted butter, very cold

¼ cup solid vegetable shortening, very cold

⅓ cup ice water

1 egg white, for egg wash

2 or 3 drops black food coloring

For the Filling

1 egg

4 egg yolks

⅔ cup granulated sugar

⅔ cup dark brown sugar, firmly packed

¼ teaspoon salt

⅓ cup heavy cream

⅓ cup whole milk

6 tablespoons salted butter, cut into small chunks

For the Topping

1 cup walnuts

Cinnamon sugar, from above

1 teaspoon vegetable oil

Continued on page 108

Continued from page 107

1. **To make the pastry:** In a large bowl, combine the flour, salt, 1 tablespoon of sugar, and ½ teaspoon of cinnamon. Cut the butter and shortening into tablespoon-size pieces and add to the flour mixture. Use a pastry cutter or 2 forks to cut into the flour. Add the water a little bit at a time and mix gently until the dough comes together.

2. On a lightly floured surface, roll out half the pastry to line the pie pan. Trim the pastry with a sharp knife to a ½-inch overhang around the edge. Fold the overhang under and crimp the edges with your fingers.

3. Roll out the other half of the dough and cut out squares 1 by 1 inch using a cookie cutter or sharp knife. Cut out at least 25 squares and place them on a baking sheet lined with a silicone baking mat or parchment paper. Chill both the pie crust and the squares for 30 minutes.

4. Toward the end of the chill time, preheat the oven to 425°F and prepare an egg wash by mixing the egg with 1 tablespoon water and a few drops of black food coloring in a small bowl. In a separate small bowl, mix the remaining 1 tablespoon sugar and the remaining 1½ teaspoons cinnamon.

5. When the pastry is done chilling, brush the squares with the egg wash and sprinkle with about half of the cinnamon sugar, reserving the remaining cinnamon sugar for the topping. Line the pie crust with foil and pie weights or dried beans and bake both the crust and squares for 10 minutes. Remove the pie pan from the oven, remove the foil and weights, and brush the bottom of the crust with the egg wash. Brush every other crimped edge with the egg wash. Return the pie pan to the oven for another 7 to 10 minutes. Keep an eye on the squares and remove them from the oven when they are crisp and starting to brown. Remove the crust from the oven and let cool. When both the pie crust and squares are baked, lower the oven temperature to 275°F and have the rack in the center of the oven.

6. **To make the filling:** In a medium heatproof bowl, whisk together the egg, egg yolks, granulated sugar, brown sugar, and salt until well combined. Whisk in the cream and milk. In a large skillet over medium-high heat, bring 1 inch of water to a boil. Turn the heat down to medium and place the bowl into the water. Scatter the butter pieces over the filling mixture and whisk until the butter is melted, and the mixture is shiny and warm to the touch.

7. Place the pie crust in the center of the oven rack and pour the filling into the crust. Bake for 45 to 50 minutes or until the edges of the filling are set but the center still has some jiggle when the pan is nudged. Remove from the oven and allow to cool completely on a wire rack. Pie should be stored in the refrigerator and can be kept for up to 3 days. Allow to come to room temperature before serving and place the baked squares on top of the pie just before serving.

8. **To make the nut topping:** In a small skillet over high heat, add the walnuts and toast for 1 minute. Turn heat down to medium. Add the remaining cinnamon sugar and the vegetable oil. Stir to combine. Continue toasting until sugar starts to liquify, stirring constantly. Remove to a plate to cool. Serve alongside the chess pie and add a bit to each bite.

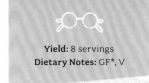
Butterscotch
ICE CREAM PIE

With butterscotch ice cream, whipped cream, and butterscotch candy, this pie might make Hermione Granger's dentist parents shudder, but the taste is magical. Inspired by the most popular wizarding drink—Butterbeer—the pie starts with a shortbread biscuit crust and ends with mouthwatering delight. Butterbeer is everywhere in the wizarding world; graphic designers Miraphora Mina and Eduardo Lima have created bottle labels for the brand for Harry Potter's time in the 1990s, and for 1920s Britain and 1930s Bhutan, seen in the Fantastic Beasts films. This recipe uses the Butterscotch Ice Cream seen on page 127 and the recipe for Shortbread Christmas Biscuits dough on page 118.

> **"Does anyone fancy
> a Butterbeer?"**
>
> —Harry Potter,
> *Harry Potter and the Half-Blood Prince*

INGREDIENTS

1½ cups shortbread biscuit crumbs, from Shortbread Christmas Biscuits (page 118)

4 tablespoons salted butter, melted

2 tablespoons sugar

⅓ cup toffee chips, divided

1 recipe Butterscotch Ice Cream (page 127), or 2 pints store bought ice cream

½ cup heavy cream

Specialty Tools
Whipped cream canister (see note)

1. In the base of a 9-inch pie plate, mix together the biscuit crumbs, melted butter, and sugar until well blended. Use your hands or another pie plate to press the crumb mixture in an even layer on the bottom and up the sides of the pie plate. Freeze for at least 1 hour.

2. While the crust is freezing, let the ice cream soften in the refrigerator.

3. Spread 2 cups ice cream into the bottom of the pie crust, sprinkle with half the toffee chips, and top with the remaining ice cream. Cover in plastic wrap and freeze for at least 2 hours or up to 2 days.

4. Reserve the remaining toffee chips in an airtight container until ready to serve.

5. About 30 minutes before serving, fill a whipped cream canister with the heavy cream. Remove the pie from the freezer, decorate the top with whipped cream rosettes, sprinkle each rosette with the remaining toffee chips, and refrigerate the pie until serving.

6. If the crust is sticking to the pie plate, place the bottom of the pie plate in warm water for about 30 seconds.

Note | If you don't have a whipped cream canister, whip the cream in a large bowl with a hand mixer until stiff peaks form. Load the whipped cream into a piping bag fitted with a large star attachment or use a large spoon to make dollops instead of rosettes.

Great Hall
FLOATING CANDLE CAKE

The Great Hall at Hogwarts is filled with light—a blazing fireplace, glowing flambeaux, and candles that float above the room, illuminating every feast and fête. The floating candles were initially produced by suspending real lights from wires, but it was quickly realized they would be better created digitally. This then allowed the computer artists to assign unique flame cycles, vary the models, and float them in arrangements that included spirals, arches, tiers, and star shapes. This chocolate cake, with a chocolate ganache filling and brown butter frosting, "burns" by a slivered almond wick to light up your dessert table.

> "Welcome to Hogwarts. Now, in a few moments, you will pass through these doors and join your classmates."
>
> —Minerva McGonagall,
> *Harry Potter and the Sorcerer's Stone*

INGREDIENTS

For the Cake
1 cup (2 sticks) unsalted butter
1½ cups light brown sugar, firmly packed
1½ cups granulated sugar
4 large eggs
1 tablespoon vanilla extract
2 cups cocoa powder
3 cups all-purpose flour
4 teaspoons baking powder
½ teaspoon salt
1⅓ cups sour cream
2 cups hot coffee

For the Filling
2 cups chopped pecans
2 teaspoons vegetable oil
2 tablespoons sugar

For the Frosting
6 egg whites
¼ teaspoon salt

2 cups dark brown sugar, firmly packed
1 teaspoon fresh lemon juice
3 cups (6 sticks) unsalted butter, cut into tablespoons, plus more for greasing
2 teaspoons vanilla extract
1 cup milk chocolate chips

For Assembly
3 wooden skewers
1 blanched almond
2 pastry bags
1 large writing tip (about #8)
1 medium writing tip (about #4)

Specialty Tools
Three 6-inch cake pans
Pastry bags and writing tips

Continued on page 112

Continued from page 111

1. **To make the cake:** Preheat the oven to 350°F. Line three 6-inch cake pans with rounds of parchment paper fitted in the bottom.

2. In the bowl of a stand mixer fitted with the paddle attachment, cream together the butter, brown sugar, and granulated sugar on medium-high speed until light and fluffy, about 3 minutes. Add the eggs and vanilla. Beat again until well combined. Add the cocoa powder and mix again until completely incorporated.

3. In a small bowl, mix together the flour, baking powder, and salt.

4. Add half of the flour mixture to the butter mixture and mix until incorporated. Scrape down the sides of the bowl and add the sour cream all at once. Mix until completely incorporated. Add the remaining flour mixture, mix again, and scrape down the sides of the bowl.

5. With the mixer running on low speed, slowly drizzle in the hot coffee. Continue to mix until all of the coffee is incorporated and batter is smooth, 2 to 3 minutes.

6. Split the batter evenly between the prepared cake pans and bake for 25 to 30 minutes, or until a cake tester inserted into the center comes out clean. Allow to cool in the pans for 15 minutes before inverting onto a wire rack and removing the parchment. Allow to cool completely.

7. Cut the dome tops off of 2 of the 3 cakes, and cut each cake into 2 even layers. Discard the cake scraps or reserve for future use. Place the layers in an airtight container between layers of parchment and freeze while you make the filling and frosting.

8. **To make the filling:** Heat a medium skillet over medium-high heat for 1 minute, add the pecans and toast, stirring continuously for 1 minute more. Turn the heat down to medium-low and add the oil and sugar. Continue stirring until most of the sugar dissolves. Transfer the pecans to a plate and allow to cool completely.

9. **To make the frosting:** Add the egg whites and salt to the bowl of a stand mixer fitted with a whisk attachment. In a medium heavy-bottomed saucepan over medium-high heat, combine the brown sugar with 1 cup of water and bring to a boil. Set the mixer on medium speed and whisk the egg whites until frothy, about 1 minute. Add the lemon juice and whisk until soft peaks form, 2 to 3 minutes more, then shut off the mixer.

10. Grease a heatproof 4-cup measuring cup with butter and set aside. Fit the saucepan with a candy thermometer and, when the sugar mixture reaches 238°F, decant it to the measuring cup.

11. Slowly add the sugar syrup to the egg whites in small batches, whisking after each addition. When all the syrup is added, beat the mixture on high speed until the meringue is completely cool (the outside of the bowl should be cool to the touch), 3 to 5 minutes.

12. Add the butter, 1 to 2 pieces at a time, beating well on medium speed after each addition. Once all the butter has been incorporated, add the vanilla and briefly beat on high speed until smooth.

13. In a medium microwave-safe bowl, add the chocolate chips. Heat for 1 minute and then let stand for 5 minutes. Stir until smooth, allow to cool for 1 to 2 minutes and then stir into 3 cups of the buttercream.

14. **To assemble the cake:** On a cake stand or small cake round, spread a bit of the chocolate buttercream and place the first layer on top. Put ½ cup of the chocolate buttercream over the top of this first layer and smooth out with an offset spatula. Sprinkle with ¼ cup of the pecan filling. Repeat these steps with the next 4 layers and then top with the 6th layer. Use any remaining chocolate frosting to seal the edges of the layers. Press 3 skewers, evenly placed, through the top layer all the way to the bottom, trimming off any excess skewer. This will ensure that this extra tall cake stays stable. Refrigerate for 30 minutes.

15. Remove the cake from the refrigerator and use an offset spatula to frost the top and sides of the cake with the buttercream. Smooth the sides, and create a low point in the middle of the top by pushing frosting toward the edges. Place about 1 cup of frosting in a pastry bag fitted with a large writing tip and pipe the "melted" rim of the candle. Use the offset spatula to smooth and sculpt this, disguising the piping and creating a wax look. Chill the cake for another 30 minutes.

16. Gently heat about a cup of frosting in the microwave, 5 to 10 seconds only. Load this frosting into a pastry bag fitted with the medium writing tip. Remove the cake from the refrigerator and use the frosting to create the "wax drips." The cold cake will stop the drips as they slide down making the candle effect.

17. Refrigerate until an hour before serving, then remove and allow to come to room temperature. Place the blanched almond as the wick in the center of the cake. The almond will light briefly if desired. The best way to cut this extra tall cake is to cut halfway down from the top, and then cut in from the side, removing slices that are 3 layers tall. Once the top has been served the bottom three layers can be cut as usual.

"I'm Sorry, Neville"
BISCUIT POPS

By using the Marauder's Map and his Invisibility
Cloak in *Harry Potter and the Prisoner of Azkaban*,
Harry makes his way into Honeydukes sweet shop
in Hogsmeade and steals a large red lollipop from
Neville Longbottom on his way through the shop. This
version is a chocolate cookie made with a peppermint
candy center that gives the shiny appearance of
stained glass. Because it was a bit unfair of Harry
to lift Neville's sweet, "I'm Sorry, Neville" is piped
around the edge in frosting in hopes of forgiveness.

> **"Why is it always me?"**
>
> —Neville Longbottom,
> *Harry Potter and the Chamber of Secrets*

Continued on page 116

Continued from page 115

INGREDIENTS

6 tablespoons salted butter, softened

2 ounces cream cheese, softened

½ cup sugar

¼ cup dark cocoa powder

1 egg

½ teaspoon peppermint extract

1½ cups all-purpose flour

About 30 unwrapped peppermint candies

About 30 lollipop sticks, optional

About 1 cup white Royal Icing from Golden Trio Biscuits (page 122)

Specialty Tools

3- and 1-inch fluted circle cookie cutters

Pastry bags and writing tips

1. Line 2 baking sheets with a silicone baking mat or parchment paper.

2. In the bowl of a stand mixer fitted with a paddle attachment, beat the butter, cream cheese, and sugar together until light and fluffy, about 3 minutes. Scrape down the sides of the bowl, add the cocoa, and mix again until well combined. Add the egg and peppermint extract and mix again.

3. Slowly add the flour, ½ cup at a time, mixing on low each time, until well combined. Form the dough into a disk, wrap it in parchment paper, and refrigerate for at least 1 hour.

4. On a lightly floured surface, roll out the dough to about ⅛ inch thick and cut out as many 3-inch circles as possible. Transfer the circles to the baking sheet, spacing out so there is enough room for the lollipop sticks, if using. Reroll the scraps and cut out more 3-inch circles. Use the 1-inch circle to cut the center out of all the large circles. You can either reroll the small circles to make more lollipops or bake them as tiny bonus biscuits.

5. Place a peppermint candy in the center of each biscuit. Gently lift the bottom of each biscuit and place a lollipop stick under the dough, just to the edge of the center hole. Gently press the dough against the stick.

6. Chill the biscuits in the refrigerator for 10 minutes. While the biscuits are chilling, preheat the oven to 350°F. Bake for 9 to 11 minutes or until the biscuits are firm and the candy has melted to fill the center.

7. Allow to cool completely on the baking sheet. Once cool they can be stored in an airtight container between layers of parchment paper for up to 5 days or wrapped in cellophane bags as favors.

8. If decorating, put the Royal icing in a pastry bag fitted with a writing tip and write, "I'm sorry, Neville!" around the candy center. Allow the icing to dry for at least 1 hour before packaging or storing. The mini center biscuits can be decorated as snowflakes.

Common Room
JAM SANDWICH BISCUITS

In the common room for Harry's first Christmas is a small evergreen tree in a pot set next to the crackling fireplace, decorated, not surprisingly, in the house colors, with miniature gold Christmas crackers, lanterns, and presents wrapped in red paper hanging from its branches. The Slytherin common room is bereft of holiday décor, but if it had any, it would be done in silver and green. These "windowed" sugar cookies, which use the Golden Trio Biscuits dough seen on page 122, can be decorated in any house's colors, like yellow and black for Hufflepuff or blue and silver for Ravenclaw. Of course, using red and green sorts you into Christmas!

> "Welcome to the Gryffindor common room. Boys' dormitory is upstairs and down to your left. Girls' the same on your right."
>
> —Percy Weasley,
> *Harry Potter and the Sorcerer's Stone*

Note | Perform a quick set test. Before you start to cook the jam, place a small plate in the freezer. After cooking the jam for at least 15 minutes, remove the plate from the freezer and put about 1 tablespoon of jam on it. When the plate is tilted, the jam should move only slowly, or barely at all. If it still runs quickly, pop the plate back into the freezer, continue to cook the jam for another 5 minutes, and check again.

INGREDIENTS

For the Sandwich Biscuits
1 recipe Golden Trio Biscuits dough, chilled, (page 122)

About ¼ cup sanding sugar, in various colors

1 jar homemade jam, see below, or store bought jam

For the Jam
4 cups crushed raspberries

3 cups granulated sugar

Juice of 1 lemon

Specialty Tools
4 clean 8-ounce jam jars with tight-fitting lids

Fluted cookie cutters, in various shapes, in 3-inch and 1½-inch sizes

1. **To make the biscuits:** Preheat the oven to 375°F. Line 2 baking sheets with silicone baking mats or parchment paper.

2. On a lightly floured surface and working with 1 disk of biscuit dough at a time, roll out the dough to ⅛ inch thick. Cut out pairs of 3-inch shapes and use their coordinating small shapes to cut a window from one biscuit of each pair. Use the edge of an offset spatula or the point of a knife to remove the small shape from the center and place it on the baking sheet. Sprinkle the windowed half, and the small biscuit, with sanding sugar, pressing it gently into the dough.

3. Repeat until you have cut out as many sets as you can. Chill in the refrigerator for at least 10 minutes before baking for 9 to 11 minutes. Repeat with the second disk.

4. **To make the jam:** If desired, run the raspberries through a food mill or press through a sieve to remove about half the seeds.

5. Add the fruit to a large saucepan and combine it with the sugar and the lemon juice. Bring to a rolling boil over high heat. Reduce to medium heat, stirring frequently, and keep at a low boil for 15 to 20 minutes or until a quick set test shows gelling (see note).

6. Remove the mixture from heat, ladle into four clean jars, and seal with tight-fitting lids. Allow the jam to cool for about 30 minutes, and then refrigerate until serving. The jam can be stored in the refrigerator for 1 month or in the freezer for 6 months. Jam makes a great gift; just be sure to label it appropriately: "Keep refrigerated for up to 1 month."

7. To serve, spread a thin layer of jam, about ½ teaspoon, onto the biscuit base, and top with its matching window. Serve right away or store in an airtight container, between layers of parchment paper, for up to 5 days.

Shortbread
CHRISTMAS BISCUITS

Shortbread is a traditional Scottish biscuit, seen everywhere around the country during the Christmas holidays. Nicknamed a "shortie," and known to be a favorite of Mary, Queen of Scots, these biscuits are a crisp and crumbly indulgence. It is never specifically mentioned in the books that Hogwarts is in Scotland, but production designer Stuart Craig decided that was where they should look for the backgrounds to the films, with its sparkling lochs and rugged mountains.

> **"I hope there's pudding."**
>
> —Luna Lovegood,
> *Harry Potter and the Order of the Phoenix*

INGREDIENTS

10 tablespoons unsalted butter

½ teaspoon sea salt

¼ cup powdered sugar

1½ tablespoons granulated sugar, divided

1½ cups all-purpose flour

Specialty Tools
8-by-8-inch baking pan

1. Prepare a bowl with an ice bath that a heatproof measuring cup will fit into. Line the baking pan with 2 strips of parchment paper that overhang the edges.

2. Add the butter to a small saucepan over medium-low heat and stir gently until the butter is melted. Continue cooking, stirring occasionally until the butter separates, turns a deep amber and smells very nutty, between 15 and 20 minutes. Transfer the butter to a heatproof measuring cup and place it in the ice bath. Let the butter cool, stirring occasionally, until it is the consistency of softened butter, about 20 minutes.

3. Preheat the oven to 300°F.

4. Transfer the brown butter to a medium bowl and add the salt, powdered sugar, and 1 tablespoon of the granulated sugar. Beat on medium speed with a hand mixer until light and fluffy, 1 to 2 minutes.

5. Sift the flour over the butter mixture, ½ cup at a time, folding it in between each addition. When all the flour has been incorporated, press the mixture into an even layer in the baking pan. Use a fork to prick the dough all over the surface.

6. Bake for 40 to 45 minutes or until a pale golden brown with slightly darker edges. Allow to cool until warm to the touch and score with a sharp knife into bars. Sprinkle with the remaining ½ tablespoon granulated sugar and allow to cool completely.

7. When completely cool, use the parchment to lift from the pan and use the score lines to cut through completely. Store in an airtight container for up to 1 week.

Golden Trio
BISCUITS

The "Golden Trio" of bespectacled Harry Potter, bushy-haired Hermione Granger, and ginger Ron Weasley are familiar faces to any Harry Potter fan, and like their characters, the three actors in their parts got along very well. Daniel Radcliffe (Harry Potter) attributes this to the fact that they were like Harry, Hermione, and Ron. He described Rupert Grint (Ron Weasley) as funny, Emma Watson (Hermione Granger) as very intelligent, and himself as being "in between," because that's how he thought of Harry. These Golden Trio Biscuits pay a sweet tribute to the undaunted heroes and fast friends.

> "Holy Cricket! You're Harry Potter. I'm Hermione Granger. And you are?"
>
> "I'm Ron Weasley."
>
> "Pleasure."
>
> —Hermione Granger and Ron Weasley, *Harry Potter and the Sorcerer's Stone*

Continued on page 122

121

Continued from page 121

INGREDIENTS

For the Dough

¾ cup salted butter, softened

4 ounces cream cheese, softened

¾ cup light brown sugar, firmly packed

1 egg

1 teaspoon vanilla

3 cups all-purpose flour

2½- to 3-inch cookie cutter

For the Royal Icing

4 cups powdered sugar, sifted

3 tablespoons meringue powder

1 to 2 drops each black, green, blue, brown, and orange food coloring

Specialty Tools

Pastry bags and writing tips

1. **To make the dough:** In a large bowl, beat together the butter, cream cheese, and sugar until light and fluffy. Add the egg and vanilla and beat again until well combined. Add the flour 1 cup at a time, mixing on low and mixing by hand with the last cup.

2. Split the dough in half, form into disks, wrap in parchment paper, and chill for at least 1 hour. Toward the end of the hour, preheat the oven to 375°F.

3. After chilling the dough, work with one half at a time on a lightly floured surface. Roll out each disk to ⅛ inch thick and cut out as many circles as you can with the cookie cutter. Transfer the rounds to a baking sheet, rewrap the scraps, and chill both the scraps and the rounds while working with the second disk.

4. Repeat with the second disk and make sure the rounds chill for at least 10 minutes before baking. Bake for 9 to 11 minutes or until just starting to brown at the edges. Allow to cool on a wire rack.

5. **To make the Royal icing:** In the bowl of a stand mixer fitted with the whisk attachment, combine the powdered sugar, meringue powder, and 6 tablespoons water. Whisk on low speed for 7 to 10 minutes, or until the icing holds stiff peaks. (If using a hand mixer, whisk on high speed for 10 to 12 minutes.)

6. Divide the icing into 5 small bowls and use the food coloring to create your desired colors. Transfer the icing to pastry bags fitted with writing tips.

7. To decorate, create each character's face on a biscuit round, starting by creating their hair across the top quarter of the biscuit and going from there. Have fun! See how many other designs you can create with just a round: Hedwig's face, Trevor the toad, a Remembrall?

8. Allow the biscuits to dry completely, at least 3 hours, before serving, packaging, or storing. Store in an airtight container between layers of parchment paper or place each biscuit in a cellophane bag for gifting.

Professor Trelawney's
POTS DE CRÈME

Pot de Crème became popular in the 17th century as a creamy sweet that was baked in a porcelain cup. This tea-infused version was inspired by the myriad teacups seen in Professor Trelawney's Divination classroom, used for the art of Tessomancy. Tessomancy predicts the future through the reading of tea leaves (although Trelawney always seems to see something negative!). There were more than 500 teacups in her room, many of these stacked on a table forming a towering china pyramid.

> "Look in the cup—tell
> me what you see!"
>
> —Sybill Trelawney,
> Harry Potter and the Prisoner of Azkaban

Note | Choose teacups without any metallic leaf décor because they can be delicate and might be damaged by the water bath.

INGREDIENTS

½ cup sugar

6 egg yolks

1½ cups whole milk

½ cup half and half

1 teaspoon vanilla extract

2 teaspoons brandy, optional

3 English breakfast tea bags (or 1 tablespoon loose leaf tea)

Specialty Tools

Six 4-ounce ramekins or teacups (see note)

Glass baking pan large enough to fit all six ramekins or teacups, lined with a clean tea towel

1. Preheat the oven to 325°F.

2. In a medium bowl, whisk together the sugar and egg yolks until well combined and pale in color.

3. In a small saucepan over medium heat, combine the milk and half and half with the vanilla, and brandy if using. Open the tea bags and stir the contents into the milk mixture. Stirring continuously, heat the milk until it comes to a simmer.

4. Remove from the heat and gradually whisk the milk into the egg mixture about ¼ cup at a time. When all the milk has been incorporated, strain the mixture through a fine mesh strainer into a heatproof measuring cup with a pour spout. Skim any foam off the top with a small spoon.

5. Split the custard evenly between the six containers and top each container with a tight-fitting piece of tin foil. Place each container in the baking pan on top of the tea towel. Place the baking pan in the oven and fill with scalding water until the level reaches halfway up the sides of the containers. Bake for 45 to 50 minutes or until set but with a bit of jiggle in the center.

6. Using a dry tea towel or tongs, carefully remove the custards from the water bath to a cooling rack and allow them to cool for 30 minutes. After 30 minutes, refrigerate for at least 2 hours before serving. These can be made up to 3 days ahead and kept, covered in the refrigerator.

Yield: 6 Servings
Dietary Notes: V

Hogsmeade
INVISIBLE SNOWBALLS

To make Harry's trip to Hogsmeade possible in *Harry Potter and the Prisoner of Azkaban*, he utilizes his Invisibility Cloak so he will not be seen. Then, when Hermione and Ron are bullied by Draco and his friends, Harry, under the cloak, peppers them with snowballs that seem to come out of thin air, frightening the Slytherin trio so much they run away. The Invisibility Cloak used by Daniel Radcliffe was constructed with green-screen material on one side that he would flip over himself to disappear or reappear. These white chocolate snowballs hide a Blondie that appears when a hot chocolate sauce is poured over the shell.

> "Who's there?"
>
> —Draco Malfoy,
> *Harry Potter and the Prisoner of Azkaban*

Continued on page 126

Continued from page 125

INGREDIENTS

For the Brownies
2 ounces white chocolate

6 tablespoons salted butter

¼ cup light brown sugar, firmly packed

½ teaspoon vanilla

2 eggs

½ cup all-purpose flour

1½ cups bittersweet chocolate chips, divided

For the Snowballs
6 ounces white chocolate

White luster dust, optional

For the Ganache
1¼ cups heavy whipping cream

¼ teaspoon cinnamon

⅛ teaspoon cayenne pepper

Specialty Tools
3-inch silicone sphere molds

1. **To make the brownie:** Preheat the oven to 350°F and prepare 3-inch silicone sphere molds by placing them on a rimmed baking sheet.

2. In a microwave-safe bowl, add 2 ounces white chocolate and the butter. Microwave for 1 minute and then stir until the butter and chocolate are completely melted. Add the sugar and stir until well combined. Add the vanilla and eggs and stir vigorously until well combined. Add the flour and stir again. Fold in ½ cup bittersweet chocolate chips.

3. Split the batter between the 6 sphere mold cavities. Bake for 15 to 20 minutes or until golden around the edges and a cake tester comes out with just a few crumbs. Cool for 10 minutes in the molds, then unmold and allow to cool completely on a wire rack.

4. **To make the snowballs:** Melt the white chocolate in a double boiler or microwave-safe bowl until just melted. Using the same molds (well cleaned and dried) and a pastry brush, dust 6 cavities with luster dust if using. Using the same brush, coat the cavities with a thin layer of chocolate. Make sure there are no blank spots, and go all the way to the edges. Place the molds in the refrigerator for 10 minutes to set.

5. **To make the ganache:** In a microwave-safe bowl, combine the cream with the remaining cup chocolate chips. Heat the mixture for 1 minute and then let stand for 5 minutes. After five minutes, stir until smooth, add the cinnamon and cayenne, and stir again. Set aside.

6. **To assemble:** Carefully remove the chocolate shells from the molds. Line a baking sheet with parchment paper. Heat a small plate in the microwave for 30 seconds and clean up the rims of each shell by twisting the edge against the warm plate, then place on parchment to cool.

7. When ready to serve, place each brownie on a small dessert plate and cover with a chocolate shell. Reheat the ganache until it is quite warm, 1 to 1½ minutes in the microwave, and give each guest a small pitcher or glass of it on the side. Each person can pour ganache over the top to melt the "snowball."

Butterscotch
ICE CREAM

A tribute to Butterbeer, this no-churn butterscotch ice cream will definitely hit your sweet spot. Ice cream is a common wizarding treat: eighty towers of No-Melt ice cream were created for the Triwizard Tournament's welcoming feast, which was made up of only puddings and desserts. The No-Melt ice cream was completely inedible, made from a combination of resin and tiny glass beads that gave it a magical iridescence as well as a credible-looking ice cream texture. This butterscotch confection is unlike the wizarding world's non-melting version, but once tasted, it probably won't last long enough to melt anyway.

> **"Three Butterbeers and some ginger and lime, please."**
>
> —Hermione Granger,
> *Harry Potter and the Half-Blood Prince*

INGREDIENTS

One 14-ounce can sweetened condensed milk

½ cup dark brown sugar, firmly packed

1 tablespoon Scotch whiskey, or whiskey extract

2 teaspoons vanilla

2½ cups heavy whipping cream

1. In a medium saucepan over medium heat, combine the sweetened condensed milk, brown sugar, whiskey and vanilla. Stir and bring to a boil. Continue boiling, stirring almost continuously for 5 to 8 minutes or until the mixture darkens and thickens considerably.

2. Remove from heat and transfer the mixture to the bowl of a stand mixer fitted with a whisk attachment. Whisk on medium-high until the sides of the bowl are completely cool. This could take up to 15 minutes. Be careful not to let your mixer overheat.

3. Stop the mixer and add the cream 1 cup at a time, mixing on low until incorporated with the butterscotch mixture. Once all the cream has been combined, increase the speed to high and mix until stiff peaks form. Stop frequently to scrape down the sides of the bowl. Transfer the mixture to an airtight container and freeze for a minimum of 6 hours or overnight.

Professor Flitwick's
CHRISTMAS FIGGY PUDDING

Figgy Pudding is a steamed cake, rather than the custardy, creamy dessert Americans know as "pudding." For Brits, however, "pudding" is an interchangeable word for dessert, though not all desserts are puddings! Figgy Pudding is a staple of the British holiday table and has been immortalized in song in the traditional Christmas carol "We Wish You A Merry Christmas." As Charms professor, Flitwick is the master of the *Wingardium Leviosa* spell and uses it to suspend Christmas ornaments onto the trees in the Great Hall in *Harry Potter and the Sorcerer's Stone*. Mixing the fruit with a bit of flour helps keep it from sinking to the bottom, staying "suspended" and evenly distributed, which illuminates the magic of baking.

INGREDIENTS

1½ cups dried figs

1½ cups all-purpose flour

1 teaspoon baking powder

2 teaspoon cinnamon

2 teaspoons ginger

½ teaspoon allspice

½ teaspoon salt

½ cup dried currants

½ cup unsalted butter, plus more for greasing

1 cup dark brown sugar, firmly packed

3 eggs

2 teaspoon vanilla extract

Whipped cream or ice cream, for serving, optional

Specialty Tools
Six 6-ounce ramekins

> "Oh, well done! See here, everyone! Ms. Granger's done it! Oh, splendid!"
>
> —Filius Flitwick,
> *Harry Potter and the Sorcerer's Stone*

1. Add the figs to a medium heatproof bowl and cover with 1 cup boiling water. Let stand for 15 minutes.

2. In a small bowl, mix together the flour, baking powder, cinnamon, ginger, allspice, and salt. Set aside.

3. Drain the figs over a bowl, reserving both the fruit and the liquid. Cut 6 figs in half and roughly chop the remaining figs. Toss the chopped figs and the currants with ¼ cup of the flour mixture. Set aside.

4. Preheat the oven to 375°F and grease the ramekins, setting them in a 9-by-13-inch casserole dish.

5. In the bowl of a stand mixer fitted with a paddle attachment, combine the butter and sugar together until light and fluffy, about 2 minutes. Add the eggs 1 at a time, mixing after each addition. Add the vanilla and mix again.

6. Add half of the remaining flour mixture and mix on low, then scrape down the sides of the bowl. Add the reserved fig liquid and mix again, ending with the remaining flour. Mix again until all the flour is incorporated. Remove the bowl from the stand mixer, scrape down the sides, and fold in the fruit.

7. Place 2 figs halves, cut side facing the bottom, into each ramekin. These will be the top of your pudding if you serve it unmolded. Split the batter between the ramekins, filling each about half full.

8. Place all the ramekins in the casserole dish, fill the pan with hot water until the water level is halfway up the ramekins, and cover the whole dish with foil. Carefully place in the oven and bake for 35 to 40 minutes or until set. Remove from the oven and transfer the ramekins to a wire rack. Serve warm in the ramekins or to unmold, run a knife around the edge of the pudding, cover with a plate, and invert to unmold. Serve with whipped cream or ice cream, if desired.

Triwizard
TRIFLE

Trifle, a layered dessert of fruits, cake, custard, and whipped cream, originated in 18th-century England according to tradition, so it has not been around as long as the 700-year-old Triwizard Tournament. This Trifle's components were inspired by the three schools that compete: Hogwarts (sponge cake), Beauxbatons (custard), and Durmstrang (lingonberry syrup). Hogwarts champions Cedric Diggory and Harry Potter grab the radiant Triwizard Cup together for the win. Inside the cup, a practical light gave it its glow. After sharing this Triwizard Trifle, your insides might glow as well.

> **"Eternal glory! That's what awaits the student who wins the Triwizard Tournament."**
>
> —Albus Dumbledore,
> *Harry Potter and the Goblet of Fire*

Continued on page 132

131

Continued from page 131

INGREDIENTS

For the Pastry Cream

½ cup sugar

3 tablespoons all-purpose flour

3 tablespoons cornstarch

6 egg yolks

2 cups whole milk

¾ teaspoon almond extract

1½ teaspoons vanilla extract

For the Cake

3 eggs

1 cup whole milk

1 tablespoon vanilla extract

2¼ cups all-purpose flour

1¼ cups sugar

4 teaspoons baking powder

½ teaspoon kosher salt

¾ cup unsalted butter, softened

For the Lingonberry Syrup

1 cup lingonberry sauce

1 cup water

¼ cup orange liqueur or orange juice

For Assembly

3 cups fresh raspberries, rinsed and drained, plus a few more for garnish

2 tablespoons powdered sugar

1½ cups heavy whipping cream

Specialty Tools

Two 6-inch cake pans

1. **To make the pastry cream:** Add the sugar, flour, cornstarch, and egg yolks to a medium bowl. Use a hand mixer, fitted with the whisk attachment, to beat on high speed until thick and light in color.

2. In a medium stainless steel saucepan, over medium-high heat, bring the milk to a simmer.

3. Remove the milk from the heat and pour about ⅓ of it into the egg mixture, stirring to combine. Transfer the milk/egg mixture back into the pan with the remaining milk and return to the stove, on medium-low heat. Whisk constantly, making sure to scrape the bottom and sides of the pan to prevent hot spots or burning. Just as the custard starts to thicken, add the almond and vanilla extracts. Continue to cook for another minute.

4. Remove from the heat and transfer into a clean bowl or airtight container. Press a piece of parchment paper against the surface of the custard to prevent a skin from forming. Allow to cool for 10 to 15 minutes. Leaving the parchment paper in place, cover the container with a lid or plastic wrap and refrigerate for at least 1 hour or up to 2 days.

5. **To make the cake:** Grease and flour the bottom of two 6-inch cake pans, or cover with parchment paper cut to fit the bottoms. Preheat the oven to 350°F.

6. Whisk the eggs in a medium bowl. Add the milk and vanilla and whisk to combine. Set aside.

7. In the bowl of a stand mixer fitted with the paddle attachment (or in a large mixing bowl using a hand mixer), combine the flour, sugar, baking powder, and salt. Mix until combined. Add the softened butter, stirring on low until a coarse crumb mixture forms.

8. Reserve ½ cup of the milk mixture and add the rest to the flour mixture. Mix on medium (or high if using a hand mixer) for about 2 minutes. Stop the mixer, add the remaining ½ cup milk, and beat for 1 minute more. Stop the mixer again, scrape down the sides of the bowl, and mix about 30 seconds more. Pour batter into the prepared cake pans, splitting the batter evenly between the 2 pans.

9. Bake for 15 to 20 minutes or until a cake tester comes out clean. Remove cakes from the oven and let cool for 15 minutes in the pan. Run an offset spatula gently around the edges of the cake pans to loosen. Cover the cake pan with a baking sheet and flip over to release the cake from the pan. Transfer to a wire rack until completely cool.

10. Trim the domed top from each cake and then cut each cake into 2 layers. For the trifle you will only need 3 of the 4 layers. Reserve the tops and the 4th layer for another purpose such as Every Flavor Cake Pops (page 91).

11. **To make the syrup:** Combine the lingonberry sauce, water, and orange liqueur in a small saucepan over medium-high heat and bring to a boil. Turn the heat down to medium-low and simmer for 1 minute. Transfer to a heatproof bowl and refrigerate until cool. Once cool, the syrup can be used right away or stored in an airtight container for up to 5 days.

12. **To assemble:** Have a large trifle bowl or glass bowl standing by.

13. Make 4 straight slices across a cake layer and then 3 the other direction, creating cubes. Lay the cake cubes in the bottom of the trifle bowl, recreating the circle, and make sure the pieces press up against the sides of the bowl.

14. Drizzle about ¼ of the lingonberry syrup over the cake and use a pastry brush to spread it out. Cover with 1 cup raspberries, spread out evenly, again touching the sides of the bowl so the layer will be visible. Use a small sieve to dust the berries with half the powdered sugar. Pour half the custard over the berries. Repeat the above set of layers again. Top with the 3rd layer of cake, brush with the remaining syrup, and top with the 3rd cup of berries, reserving a few raspberries for garnish. Cover and refrigerate while you whip the cream.

15. In a large bowl or in the bowl of a stand mixer fitted with a whisk attachment, whisk the cream on high just until stiff peaks form. Remove the trifle from the refrigerator, and gently spoon the whipped cream over the berries and use an offset spatula to spread into an even layer. Garnish with more berries and refrigerate for at least 3 hours or overnight.

Note | The trifle can be made up to 24 hours ahead and leftovers can be kept, covered in the refrigerator, for up to 2 days.

DRINKS

Hot Chocolate
BROOMS

Brooms are ubiquitous in the wizarding world. For the films, these needed to be incredibly durable, so an aircraft grade titanium center was covered by mahogany wood, then birch branches were added for the bristle head. Some brooms were customized for their character: Tonks's broom had multicolored branches in the head; Arthur Weasley's had a bicycle basket on it. These wood-handled spoon "brooms" have a "bristle head" of semisweet chocolate, cocoa, and sugar that creates a warming drink you can customize with crushed peppermints, mini marshmallows, or whipped cream.

> **"That's not just any broomstick, Harry. It's a Nimbus 2000!"**
>
> —Ron Weasley,
> *Harry Potter and the Sorcerer's Stone*

INGREDIENTS

2 cups semisweet chocolate chips, divided

½ cup unsweetened cocoa powder

2½ tablespoons sugar

2 tablespoons heavy whipping cream

8 flat handled wooden spoons

1. Line a baking sheet with parchment paper.
2. In a microwave-safe bowl, melt 1 cup chocolate chips in 30 second bursts, stirring until melted. Add the cocoa powder, sugar, and cream and stir until combined and a thick paste forms.
3. Mold about 2 tablespoons of the mixture around the bowl of each of the wooden spoons, creating a broom shape. Press the shape against the baking sheet to create a flat, stable bottom. Refrigerate for 20 minutes.
4. Melt the remaining 1 cup chocolate chips, as above. Remove the brooms from the refrigerator and dip each one in the melted chocolate, using an offset spatula to make sure the whole broom is covered and sealed to the spoon handle. Use the tines of a fork to drag the chocolate and create the broom's texture. Place back on the baking sheet, standing upright, and repeat with the remaining spoons. Chill for 10 minutes or until set.
5. To serve, pour 8 ounces very hot milk, or non-dairy beverage of choice, into a mug. Place a broom in the mug, let stand for 2 minutes, and then stir!
6. Make sure to have plenty of toppings on hand, such as mini marshmallows, peppermint chips, and whipped cream.
7. The brooms can be stored in an airtight container for up to 2 weeks or packaged in cellophane bags for gift giving. If desired, use a fine tip pen to write on the broom handles, personalize with the names of the recipients, Nimbus 2000, Nimbus 2001, Firebolt, or Quidditch World Cup.

Yield: 4 servings
Dietary Notes: GF, V, V+*

Hogwarts
PUNCH

In *Harry Potter and the Goblet of Fire*, one thing many of the students look forward to during the Triwizard Tournament is the Yule Ball that takes place over the Christmas holiday. Tables were set with food and beverages, the drinks served from two cauldron-shaped punch bowls that bracketed an icy centerpiece. Beverages were also available in long-necked bottles etched with snowflakes that contained one of four pastel-colored liquids representing Hogwarts' four houses. This Hogwarts punch honors the two winners of the tournament—Hufflepuff Cedric Diggory and Gryffindor Harry Potter—with its yellowy golden hue. This, Durmstrang Punch (page 141), and Beauxbatons Punch (page 143) are small batches meant to be served as a trio to create twelve servings. They are easily doubled or even tripled to create larger batches.

INGREDIENTS

4 cups lemonade

½ cup apricot nectar

3 to 4 sprigs fresh thyme, plus more for garnish

2 tablespoons honey

½ lemon, thinly sliced for garnish

¼ teaspoon gold luster dust, optional

1. In a medium saucepan, combine the lemonade, apricot nectar, thyme, and honey over medium heat. Bring to a low boil, remove from heat, and allow to steep for 30 minutes. Strain through a fine mesh sieve into a wide mouth measuring cup or pitcher with a pour spout, and chill until serving.

2. To serve, pour into a large pitcher or punch bowl. Stir in luster dust, if using, and float the lemon slices and thyme sprigs in the punch.

Note | For a vegan option, use agave instead of honey.

> **"I just wondered if maybe you wanted to go to the ball with me?"**
>
> —Harry Potter to Cho Chang,
> *Harry Potter and the Goblet of Fire*

Yield: 4 servings
Dietary Notes: GF, V, V+

Durmstrang
PUNCH

Any punch that would represent Durmstrang Institute would need to be fiery, bringing to mind the fire-breathers that announce the entrance of these students into the Great Hall for the Triwizard Tournament. The color red is also prominent on their military-style uniforms, which bear the double-headed eagle, the symbol for the school. And for the Yule Ball, the Durmstrang men stood out in bright red coats with talon-shaped fasteners and a fur-lined half cape that unfurled as they swung their partners around in the dance. With black peppercorns and ginger for zing, and cherry and apple juices for sweetness, this punch will make you flip like the proud sons of Durmstrang.

> "And now our friends from the North—please greet the proud sons of Durmstrang."
>
> —Albus Dumbledore,
> *Harry Potter and the Goblet of Fire*

INGREDIENTS

2 cups apple juice

1 bay leaf

One 3-inch piece ginger, peeled and thinly sliced

1 tablespoon black peppercorns

2 cups unsweetened cherry juice

¼ teaspoon silver luster dust, optional

Fresh bay leaves, for garnish, optional

1. In a medium saucepan over medium heat, combine the apple juice, bay leaf, ginger slices, and peppercorns. Bring to a boil then remove from the heat and allow to steep for 30 minutes. Strain through a fine mesh strainer into a measuring cup with a pour spout.

2. Combine the infused apple juice with the cherry juice in a measuring cup with a pour spout and chill until ready to serve.

3. To serve, pour into a large pitcher or punch bowl and garnish with fresh bay leaves, if using. Stir in the luster dust, if using.

Note | This punch is also delicious served warm. These are small batch punches meant to be served as a trio to create 12 servings. They are easily doubled or even tripled to create larger batches.

Beauxbatons
PUNCH

The lovely ladies of Beauxbatons Academy have a chic nature that balances with the steel in their spines. With the same style, this fragrant punch combines the calming earthy undertones of lavender with the crispness of sparkling white grape juice for a refreshing drink that epitomizes the sophisticated students. Costume designer Jany Temime, being French herself, chose the classic "French blue" color for the Beauxbatons girls' outfits, but for the Yule Ball, she wanted something that better reflected the culture and couture of her country. To show unity among the students, the Beauxbatons were dressed in gray-blue gowns, with thirty meters (ninety feet) of chiffon in Fleur Delacour's gown alone!

> "Please join me in welcoming the lovely ladies of Beauxbatons Academy of Magic ..."
>
> —Albus Dumbledore,
> *Harry Potter and the Goblet of Fire*

INGREDIENTS

½ cup sugar

2 teaspoons dried culinary lavender

1 to 2 drops light blue food coloring

¼ teaspoon periwinkle blue luster dust, optional

4 cups sparkling white grape juice, chilled

Fresh lavender sprigs, for garnish, optional

1. In a small saucepan, over medium heat, bring the sugar and 1 cup water to a boil, stirring until the sugar is completely dissolved. Remove from the heat and stir in the lavender. Allow to steep for 30 minutes.

2. Strain through a fine mesh strainer into a measuring cup with a pour spout, add the food coloring and luster dust, if using. Store in an airtight container in the refrigerator until ready to serve.

3. To serve, combine the lavender syrup and the sparkling grape juice, by gently stirring them into a large pitcher or punch bowl. Float lavender sprigs in the punch, if using.

Note | These are small batch punches meant to be served as a trio to create 12 servings. They are easily doubled or even tripled to create larger batches.

Yield: 4 servings
Dietary Notes: GF, V, V+

Professor Trelawney's
FORTIFIED EARL GREY TEA

Tessomancy is the art of reading tea leaves, which is the first lesson Professor Sybill Trelawney teaches in her third years' initial Divination class. Ron interprets Harry's tea leaves as that he will suffer, but he'll be happy about it. When Trelawney looks at it, she sees the "Grim," an omen of death. Of course, she sees something negative in every cup she views. This drink is nothing but positives: the bold flavor of Earl Grey tea, a lemony simple syrup, and the fortification of a nice dry gin.

> **"Broaden your mind!"**
> —Sybill Trelawney,
> *Harry Potter and the Prisoner of Azkaban*

INGREDIENTS

For the Lemon Simple Syrup
3 lemons
1 cup sugar

For the Tea
2 Earl Grey tea bags

4 ounces lemon simple syrup

8 ounces fresh squeezed lemon juice

8 ounces gin

4 lemon slices, for garnish

1. **To make the lemon simple syrup:** Use a vegetable peeler or paring knife to remove the rind from the lemons, leaving behind as much pith as possible. Reserve the lemons for juicing.

2. Add the lemon rind to a small saucepan with 1 cup water and the sugar. Bring to a boil over medium heat, and stir until the sugar is completely dissolved, about 1 minute. Remove from heat, allow to cool, and store in an airtight container in the refrigerator for up to 1 week.

3. **To make the tea:** In a heatproof measuring cup or mug, combine the teabags with 8 ounces of boiling water and allow to steep for 6 minutes. Remove the teabags and chill the tea in the refrigerator until serving.

4. To serve, fill a cocktail pitcher halfway with ice, add the tea, lemon simple syrup, lemon juice, and gin.

5. Stir until well chilled, then pour through a strainer into teacups or glasses. Garnish with a lemon slice.

Cast a Christmas Spell
SPICED CIDER

Spiced cider is a classic holiday beverage, served all through the Christmas season. Its origins have been thought to trace back to another drink known as wassail, made from roasted apples and sung about in a popular Christmas carol. Ghostly carolers sing a Hogwarts ode to the holiday, called "Ring the Hogwarts Bell," in *Harry Potter and the Sorcerer's Stone*. Dressed in Dickensian-type outfits, they fill the halls with this song as students leave for the holiday. This hot and fruity spiced cider would be the perfect drink to end any winter's day, whether you're caroling or just Christmas-ing.

> "Merry Christmas,
> Merry Christmas
>
> **Ring the Hogwarts bell!**
>
> Merry Christmas,
> Merry Christmas
>
> **Cast a Christmas spell!"**
>
> —Hogwarts Ghostly Carolers,
> *Harry Potter and the Sorcerer's Stone*

Note | This recipe can easily be doubled for a larger crowd. Slow cookers are ideal for mulled drinks because they cook at a low and constant temperature.

INGREDIENTS

2 apples, divided

2 oranges, divided

1 tablespoon whole cloves

½ gallon unfiltered apple cider

4 tablespoons brown sugar

4 cinnamon sticks

2 whole star anise

⅛ teaspoon nutmeg

1. Slice one of the apples into thin round slices and gently remove seeds. Reserve the second apple for garnish.

2. Slice one orange in half lengthwise, then slice each half into thin slices. Reserve the second orange for garnish.

3. Poke the cloves into the end slices of orange so they can be easily removed from the mixture, or place them in a tea infuser.

4. **Slow cooker method:** Add the cider, sugar, sliced apple, sliced orange, cloves, cinnamon, star anise, and nutmeg to the slow cooker, and heat for 1 to 1½ hours on low, stirring halfway through.

5. **Stove top method:** Add 4 cups of the cider and the sugar to a large pot over medium-low heat. Cook, stirring occasionally, until the sugar dissolves and cider is at a low boil. Lower heat to low and add remaining cider, sliced apple, sliced orange, cloves, cinnamon, star anise, and nutmeg. Bring back to a simmer over low heat and cook for 30 to 45 minutes. Turn off heat, stir, and allow to sit for 10 to 15 minutes.

6. Serve cider warm in mugs with fresh fruit sliced as above. Add one piece each to the mugs.

7. Cider can be stored in an airtight container in the refrigerator, for 1 to 2 days. Be sure to remove the fruit and whole spices before storing, so the spice level does not become too strong and fruit does not ferment. Reheat in the slow cooker or in a large pot over medium heat before serving.

Yield: 2 servings
Dietary Notes: GF, V, V+

HAIR OF THE CAT

To discover the identity of the Heir of Slytherin, who has unleashed the deadly Basilisk upon Muggle-borns at Hogwarts in *Harry Potter and the Chamber of Secrets*, Hermione concocts Polyjuice Potion for transformations using hairs from Crabbe and Goyle that will allow Harry and Ron to enter the Slytherin dormitory. Hermione, regrettably, took cat hairs off Slytherin Millicent Bulstrode's robes and transformed into a human/cat hybrid, so she could not go. As the special effects team wanted the potion to look and taste as disgusting as possible, it was made of lumps of vegetable and different colored edible dyes, and the drink was served cold to garner a real reaction from the actors. This drink, inspired by that moment, blends tropical kiwis, lime, and coconut that will give the real reaction of delight to this exotic brew.

INGREDIENTS

2 ripe kiwis

2 cups coconut water, chilled

2 teaspoons chia seeds

1 lime, divided

⅛ teaspoon green luster dust, optional

4 tablespoons shredded coconut, toasted

1. Peel and core the kiwis and add the flesh to the pitcher of a blender. Add the coconut water and blend on high until the kiwi is puréed. Transfer the mixture to an airtight container and add the chia seeds, juice of half the lime, and luster dust if using. Stir to combine. Cover and refrigerate for 15 to 20 minutes or until thickened.

2. Just before serving cut the remaining lime half in half and use the quarters to wet the rims of 2 glasses.

3. Pour the toasted coconut onto a shallow plate, and twist the rims of the glasses in the coconut to coat.

4. Split the mixture between the two glasses and serve immediately.

> "Look at my face."
>
> "Look at your tail!"
>
> —Hermione Granger and Ron Weasley,
> *Harry Potter and the Chamber of Secrets*

Yield: 6 servings
Dietary Notes: GF, V, V+*

Magical
MULLED WINE

To mull something means to heat it, sweeten it, and flavor it with spices, something revelers in the British Isles have been doing for centuries. This heartening drink features the sweetness of oranges and honey, the licorice-y tang of star anise, and a generous dollop of brandy for heat. It not only tastes good, but its colors also look great at any Christmas party. Mead was historically created by the Romans who occupied the colder European regions; not only did it warm them up, it had health benefits as well due to the fruits and spices. Mulled wine is very similar to mead, a bottle of which Horace Slughorn shares with Harry and Ron, but they discover it has been poisoned when Ron falls ill. Mulled wine would have been much healthier!

> **"Here, old boy. Bottom's up!"**
>
> —Horace Slughorn,
> *Harry Potter and the Half-Blood Prince*

INGREDIENTS

3 clementine oranges, divided

1 tablespoon whole cloves

One 750 milliliter bottle of dry red wine

1 cup orange juice

½ cup honey

2 tablespoon brown sugar

4 sticks cinnamon

2 whole star anise

1 bay leaf

⅛ teaspoon allspice

¼ cup brandy, optional

1. Slice 2 of the clementines into three thick slices each. Reserve the remaining clementine for garnish.

2. Poke the cloves into the ends of the oranges so they can be removed from the mixture easily, or place in a tea infuser.

3. **Slow cooker method:** Add the wine, sliced oranges, orange juice, honey, brown sugar, cinnamon, star anise, bay leaf, allspice, and brandy, and stir gently to combine. Cook on low for 1½ hours. Use a slotted spoon to remove the oranges and whole spices.

4. **Stove top method:** In a large pot over medium heat, add the orange juice, honey, and sugar, and bring to a low boil until sugar and honey dissolve. Add the wine, oranges, cinnamon, star anise, bay leaf, allspice, and brandy. Bring back to a simmer then lower heat to low, and cook for 30 minutes. Use a slotted spoon to remove the oranges and whole spices.

5. Serve hot in mugs with fresh clementine sliced rounds floating in each mug.

6. Mulled wine can be stored in an airtight container in the refrigerator, for 1 to 2 days. Be sure to remove the oranges and whole spices before storing, so the spice level does not become too strong and fruit does not ferment. Gently reheat in the slow cooker or in a large pot over medium-low heat, until desired temperature, before serving, but do not re-boil.

Note | For a vegan version, swap the honey for agave. The spices and fruit will be adding so much flavor that an expensive wine is not necessary. Inexpensive Cabernet, Zinfandel, or Malbec is ideal.

Mistletoe
COCKTAIL

Yield: 2 servings
Dietary Notes: GF, V, V

Harry Potter experiences his first kiss with Cho Chang after the students in Dumbledore's Army leave for the Christmas holiday in *Harry Potter and the Order of the Phoenix*. He's had a crush on her for a while, and the two finally express their feelings when Cho points out that they're standing underneath a sprig of mistletoe. Both Daniel Radcliffe and Katie Leung were nervous before the scene was filmed. Radcliffe remembers "lots of courtesy gum chewing that day." The edible mint leaves in this cocktail represent the inedible mistletoe, and ought to ensure that any smooch should be a success.

INGREDIENTS

5 to 6 mint leaves, plus more for garnish

4 ounces coconut milk

1 ounce simple syrup, plus more for garnish

2 ounces lime juice

4 ounces white rum

2 ounces coconut water

1 tablespoon superfine sugar, for garnish

1. In a cocktail shaker, muddle together the mint, coconut milk, and simple syrup. Add five or six ice cubes to the cocktail shaker and top off with the lime juice, rum, and coconut water.

2. Fill two highball glasses halfway with ice.

3. Shake until the cocktail shaker is frosted over. Strain between the two glasses. Garnish with sugared mint leaves (see note).

Note | To make sugared mint leaves, mix 1 teaspoon simple syrup with 1 teaspoon water until thoroughly combined. Use a pastry brush to apply a very thin layer of simple syrup mixture onto the leaves of two short mint sprigs. Sprinkle with sugar and set aside on a plate to dry until needed. To garnish the cocktail, place a cocktail stick across the top of the glass and hang the sugared mint upside down over the cocktail stick, like mistletoe.

"Mistletoe."

"Probably full of Nargles, though"

—Cho Chang and Harry Potter,
Harry Potter and the Order of the Phoenix

Yield: 1 serving
Dietary Notes: V, GF

PUMPKIN FIZZ

Pumpkins are prevalent in the wizarding world: Pumpkin Juice (a popular drink among the Hogwarts students) and pumpkins that hang over the tables of the Great Hall at Halloween. There's a pumpkin patch next to Hagrid's hut, and there are even pumpkin-shaped chocolate cakes, served at the welcoming feast for the Triwizard Tournament. Interestingly, a few of the prop pumpkins in Hagrid's pumpkin patch were used to make the molds for the chocolate cakes. The sweetness of apple juice combines with the spicy kicks of pumpkin butter and gingery bubbles for a lip-smacking iced fizzy drink.

> "You'll find no small glasses in this house."
>
> —Rubeus Hagrid,
> *Harry Potter and the Prisoner of Azkaban*

INGREDIENTS

For the Pumpkin Butter
3 pounds winter squash, such as sugar pie, Jarrahdale, winter luxury, or butternut

1 cup apple juice, divided

2 tablespoons bourbon or vanilla extract

1 cup dark brown sugar

1 teaspoon ground cinnamon

¼ teaspoon ground clove

For the Pumpkin Fizz
3 tablespoons apple juice

2 tablespoons pumpkin butter (or store bought)

6 to 8 ounces ginger beer or ginger ale

Specialty Tools
Eight 4-ounce or four 8-ounce jars

1. **To make the pumpkin butter:** Have ready eight 4-ounce or four 8-ounce jars with tight-fitting lids, well washed or sterilized. Preheat the oven to 350°F.

2. Halve each squash and scoop out the seeds and stringy pulp. Cut the stem end off and discard it.

3. Pour ½ cup of the apple juice with ½ cup water into a roasting pan. Place the squash pieces, cut side down, in the pan and roast for 45 to 50 minutes, or until very tender when poked with a fork.

4. Allow the squash to cool for 10 minutes, then use a fork and spoon to scrape the flesh from the skin.

5. Place all the flesh and the cooking liquid in a large heavy-bottomed saucepan. Discard the skin.

6. Add the remaining ½ cup of apple juice, the bourbon, brown sugar, cinnamon, and clove. Place over medium heat and cook, stirring, until the mixture begins to bubble, about 10 minutes. Turn the heat down to low, cover partially, and simmer for 20 to 25 minutes, or until the mixture clings to a spoon for several seconds before falling back in the pot.

7. Remove from the heat and use an immersion blender to purée into a smooth texture. Immediately fill the clean jars and seal with tight-fitting lids. Allow to cool to room temperature and then refrigerate. The pumpkin butter will store in the refrigerator for up to three weeks.

8. **To make the fizz:** In a tall glass, mix the apple juice and pumpkin butter together until smooth. Fill the glass with ice and top off with ginger beer or ginger ale. Stir gently to combine or serve layered, with a spoon or straw.

Black Lake
SIMPLE SYRUP

A simple syrup sweetens any beverage by the simple act of combining equal parts sugar and water, heating it so the sugar dissolves, and then adding it to iced drinks or cocktails. It can also be flavored by adding other ingredients, such as, with this Black Lake—inspired version, black cocoa powder. The Black Lake is aptly named—it's hard to see anything under its murky waters, as Harry learns during the second task of the Triwizard Tournament in *Harry Potter and the Goblet of Fire*. Black Lake Simple Syrup can be mixed with sparkling wine for a dark mimosa, added to ginger ale, or used to create a Black and Orange (page 155). This simple syrup will make any drink darker and sweeter, simply.

INGREDIENTS

1 cup sugar

1 tablespoon black cocoa powder

1. In a small saucepan over medium-high heat, combine the sugar with 1 cup water. Bring to a boil, stirring continuously until all the sugar is dissolved, about 1 minute.

2. Remove from the heat, allow to cool for 15 minutes, and whisk in the cocoa powder until the mixture is smooth and no lumps remain. Keep in an airtight container in the refrigerator for up to 1 week.

Yield: 4 servings
Dietary Notes: GF, V, V+

BLACK AND ORANGE

A Black and Tan is a popular British cocktail that combines a dark and a light beer that separate due to the different densities in the drinks. This "black and orange" version gives it a wizarding twist, layering in the sweet Black Lake Simple Syrup (page 154) and full-bodied piquancy of a Pumpkin Fizz.

> "Myrtle, there aren't merpeople in the Black Lake are there?"
>
> —Harry Potter,
> *Harry Potter and the Goblet of Fire*

INGREDIENTS

2 tablespoon Black Lake Simple Syrup (page 154)

3 tablespoons apple juice

2 tablespoon pumpkin butter

6 to 8 ounces ginger beer or ginger ale

1. Pour the simple syrup into the bottom of a large glass, being careful not to get it on the side.

2. In a small bowl, combine the apple juice and pumpkin butter together until smooth.

3. Fill the glass with ice and pour the apple juice mixture over it. Let the layers settle a minute and then top with ginger beer or ginger ale by slowly pouring it over the back of a spoon. Serve immediately with a spoon or straw for stirring.

Yield: 1 serving
Dietary Notes: GF

THE GREY LADY

In *Harry Potter and the Deathly Hallows — Part 2*, it was learned that the ghost of Ravenclaw house, the Grey Lady, was actually the daughter of Rowena Ravenclaw. Rowena, the Ravenclaw house founder, wore a diadem that Voldemort turned into a Horcrux. The diadem, designed by Miraphora Mina, features the Ravenclaw eagle in blue stones surrounded by white drops and the Ravenclaw house motto. This drink visually references the sparkle of the Diadem with a glistening sugar rim and the ghostly presence of the Grey Lady with a bluish gray liquid color.

> "**Wit beyond measure is man's greatest treasure.**"
>
> —Ravenclaw house motto

INGREDIENTS

For the Blue Simple Syrup
1 cup sugar

1 tablespoon
butterfly pea flowers

For the Drink
2 tablespoons dark
blue sanding sugar

½ tablespoon blue simple syrup

3 blackberries, divided

1 teaspoon meringue powder

2 ounces vodka

1 ounce St. Germain,
or elderflower liqueur

Specialty Tools
Coupe glass

1. **To make the blue simple syrup:** In a small saucepan combine the sugar with 1 cup water and bring to a boil over medium-high heat. Stir continuously until the sugar is completely dissolved. Remove from the heat, stir in the flowers, and allow to steep until completely cool, about 1 hour. Strain through a fine mesh strainer into an airtight container and store the syrup in the refrigerator for up to 1 week.

2. **To make the drink:** Place the sanding sugar in a shallow dish. Rim the cocktail glass with a bit of simple syrup and place the glass, rim edge down, in the sugar, give it a twist until the entire rim is covered in sugar. Press 1 blackberry against the edge of the glass to hold.

3. Muddle the remaining 2 blackberries and blue simple syrup in the bottom of a cocktail shaker. Add the meringue powder, vodka, and St. Germain. Add a few ice cubes, leaving plenty of room to create froth. Shake vigorously until the cocktail shaker frosts, over and strain into the coupe glass. Serve immediately.

Note | Food coloring can be used instead of the butterfly pea flowers in the blue simple syrup, but it does not have the same color changing magic as the butterfly pea flower and will affect the color of your cocktail.

HARRY POTTER

HOLIDAY-THEMED PARTIES

"On Christmas Eve night, we and our guests gather in
the Great Hall for a night of well-mannered frivolity."

—Minerva McGonagall, *Harry Potter and the Goblet of Fire*

PARTY PLANNING
AND SUGGESTED MENUS

Is there anything better than gathering friends and family for a party with great food and drink, lively conversation, and bright and colorful decorations? Well, we think there is—when the party is themed to the amazing wizarding world films that feature Harry Potter, Ron Weasley, and Hermione Granger, among many fascinating witches and wizards.

But holiday parties don't just appear with a wave of your wand. Every party takes time, hard work, and attention to detail to make it unique and memorable, for both the party guests and the party giver. The filmmakers served 450 students in the Welcome Feast in *Harry Potter and the Sorcerer's Stone*, but for your first time hosting a wizarding bash, you might want to aim for a smaller number of guests. The type of party you host can be an elaborate dance party like the Yule Ball in *Harry Potter and the Goblet of Fire* or a cozy cocktail party similar to the Slug Club Christmas gathering in *Harry Potter and the Half-Blood Prince*.

There's a lot to consider when planning a party, especially your table scape, including dinnerware, linens, serving dishes, cutlery, and table covers. Hogwarts uses gold plates and flatware at all its mealtimes. Set out place cards if you'd like and add a centerpiece or two to the table. Horace Slughorn used red lanterns, and the Weasleys had Christmas crackers and holiday cards strewn around Grimmauld Place during their Christmas there.

Setting the scene is important and decorations are key: Trees, ornaments, garlands, and twinkling lights will bring magic to your get-together. You can decorate your Christmas tree with a gold star or a gold gnome as the topper, and feature large and small gold stars, crescent moons, long-tailed partridges, and glittering orbs similar to the ones Professor Flitwick levitated onto the Great Hall's trees using *Wingardium Leviosa*. Or decorate the tree in your house colors: in Harry's first year, Gryffindor's Christmas tree featured gold Christmas crackers (an English Christmas tradition) and miniature, red-colored gift boxes.

If you're not able to have a tree, you can drape bowers of evergreen branches on shelves or over doors and decorate them with golden pine cones or other ornaments. You can also hang wreaths from doors or the walls. The smell of pine or fir will add to the Christmas ambience of your party. Stream a crackling fireplace on your TV or any monitor if you don't have a fireplace yourself and hang some mistletoe in the room (just watch out for Nargles!).

Food really sets the flavor of any party, and a party with a specific theme such as "Christmas in the Wizarding World" lends itself to an iconic menu. Traditional English fare features roast meats and vegetables, or you can have savory seafood or curries. Or, like the Welcome Feast for the Triwizard Tournament in *Harry Potter and the Goblet of Fire*, you can serve only desserts! Hors d'oeuvres can range from the sweet to the salty, and there's nothing like a Hot Chocolate Broom or Magical Mulled Wine in the chilly season.

Festive activities can include caroling, exchanging presents, hanging Christmas cards or paper snowflakes in a red-and-gold or silver-and-green twisted garland around your living space, or making Christmas crackers and spirals of gold tinsel with which you can decorate the tree.

You can even put together your own version of the Yule Ball, with a program of events, such as a demonstration of wand moves. Dancing would be in order; you can distribute a card before the event with a dance tutorial (make sure you label right and left feet correctly!). The Yule Ball seen in *Harry Potter and the Goblet of Fire* featured silver plates and flatware and crystal-cut glasses; tablecloths, chairs, and everything else in the room was draped in silver fabric. Punch can be served in a cauldron-shaped bowl, and fake snow can be sprayed on trees or pine boughs. Be sure to "dress to impress," as is written on the original Yule Ball invitation. (Design your own dress robes but avoid any advice on this from Ron's Great-Aunt Tessie!)

Celebrate a wizarding world Christmas at any time of the year. Spray fake removable snow on your windows and wear your wool house scarf inside. Play carols in the background while you cook mouthwatering feasts and bake sumptuous desserts. Any time is the right time to have a happy Christmas.

White Erumpent
GIFT EXCHANGE

A White Elephant is a gift exchange where participants can swap around gifts they pull out of a sack, hoping to walk away with the best one in the bag, rather than the worst, which is referred to as the white elephant. Those in the wizarding world might call it a White Erumpent Gift Exchange. In this version, everyone brings a Harry Potter–themed gift and the host puts a Holiday Fruitcake they've made to act as the White Erumpent. First, everyone draws a number, and the gifts are chosen in that order. You can either choose a new gift from the bag, or "steal" a gift from someone who has gone before. Note however that a gift can only be stolen once per round. But once a gift has been passed between 3 people, the third owner gets to keep the gift and it can no longer be stolen. The magic here is that whoever gets the fruitcake will be the winner because it will be delicious!

Yule Ball
PARTY MENU

Hogwarts students receive an invitation requesting the pleasure of their company to celebrate Christmas and the Triwizard Tournament at the Yule Ball, where beverages and a Yule Feast are served, a Witch and Wizard of the Ball are announced, and there's a Yule Parade of Wand Skills. This menu will complement a "night of well-mannered frivolity" with colorful punches, succulent fish dishes, and a creamy, fruity layered confection.

Slug Club
COCKTAIL PARTY MENU

Professor Horace Slughorn hosts several parties during the events of *Harry Potter and the Half-Blood Prince*. At his Christmas party, he gathers together the most recent Slug Club members with those witches and wizards he's stayed in touch with over the years. A cocktail party is a wonderful occasion for new friends and old to meet and enjoy an intimate holiday gathering. There's a wide variety of tastes and textures in this suggested menu; there are nutty and fruity, as well as fiery and cool selections, all of which will charm your guests.

MOVIE NIGHT
Around the Fire Menu

On a cold winter's night, there's nothing better than getting together to watch a favorite movie or two with film fans and companions. This Movie Night around the Fire menu is filled with entertaining comfort food that will warm viewers from head to toe even if there isn't a fireplace nearby. A visit to Hogwarts by watching the Harry Potter films can easily provide a substitute, from the huge fireplace in the Gryffindor common room to the blazing fire and flambeaux in the Great Hall of Hogwarts.

Grimmauld Place
CHRISTMAS EVE MENU

Christmas Eve is a time of great fun and anticipation—
who will be there, what stories will everyone tell,
and what will my presents be tomorrow? (If you're a
Weasley, it's pretty sure you'll get something knitted
from Molly!) It's a good idea to have a hearty, grounding
menu for the eve before the Christmas holiday and
this very special dinner offers a nod toward tradition
and a wink (as Sirius did to Harry) at the future.

CHRISTMAS DAY MENU

If there is one thing Muggles and wizards have in common, it's the love of being with family and friends to celebrate Christmas. During this time, Hogwarts is decorated with fragrant trees and wreaths, thoughtful presents are exchanged, and everyone gathers together around the table to feast on crisp greens, juicy meats, and hearty breads. And then there's always a spectacular dessert that heightens the sweetness of the holiday. A Christmas Day menu such as this one is sure to make for magical merriment.

BOXING DAY
Get-Together Menu

Boxing Day is the day after Christmas, a perfect time to visit those who had their own family or friends Christmas feasts and exchange gifts. Gifts that come in boxes, of course, but you can also get together and gift those you care about with an array of giftable treats. These recipes are a gift as well—they use up any leftovers from Christmas Day, are great for a brunch-type celebration, and are tremendously tasty.

GLOSSARY

Deglaze: Deglazing is adding liquid, usually wine or stock, to a hot pan to release all the caramelized food from the pan. These caramelized bits, called fond, are full of flavor and should not be left behind. Deglazing is often the first step in making a delicious sauce.

Egg Wash: Whisk together 1 egg and 1 tablespoon of water until light and foamy. Use a pastry brush to apply when the recipe requires.

High-Heat vs. Nonstick Pans: Many recipes in the book call for high-heat pans. Typically, this would mean stainless steel, cast iron, or enameled cast iron. Stove temperatures are based on these types of cookware. If you are cooking with nonstick cookware, please make sure that you know the manufacturer's heat limits for your cookware. Most nonstick cookware should not be used at above medium heat on a stove and is not suitable for the oven. Cooking times may need to be adjusted to account for this.

Luster Dust: This dust is a food-safe glitter that can be purchased online or in specialty baking departments. It can be mixed with clear alcohol to create a shimmery paint or brushed on dry.

Milk: The word milk in this book is always referring to dairy milk unless otherwise noted. In most cases any percentage of milk fat will do unless otherwise noted.

Peeling Ginger: The easiest way to peel fresh ginger is with a small spoon. Simply use the edge of the spoon to scrape away the peel. This keeps the ginger root intact, with less waste, and allows you to easily navigate all the bumps and lumps.

Salt: Feel free to use your salt of choice unless it has been noted in the recipe. Kosher salt is the one most commonly used throughout the book.

Silicone Baking Mat: Silicone baking mats can be used up to high temperatures in the oven and used in the freezer. They are very helpful in baking because you can easily roll dough out on them and then take them from prep station to chilling to oven without having to move dough. They are extremely nonstick and easy to clean.

Sumac: Made from ground berries of the sumac flower. It has a sour and slightly acidic taste and is most commonly used in Mediterranean and Middle Eastern cooking. It is great for dry rubs, marinades, and even dressings. It adds a great punch of flavor and color.

Vanilla Paste vs. Vanilla Extract: Vanilla bean paste can give you the strong vanilla flavor and the beautiful vanilla bean flecks without having to split and steep a vanilla bean. While it is more expensive than extract, there are recipes where it will really shine and elevate a dish. When it will make a wonderful addition to a dish it has been called out, but it can always be replaced with vanilla extract with a 1-for-1 swap out.

DIETARY CONSIDERATIONS

Breakfasts

Restricted Section Puff Pastry Books .... **V**
Granola Breakfast of
Triwizard Champions .... **GF*, V, V+***
Snape's Bubble and Squeak .... **GF, V***
Neville's Toad in the Hole
The Chosen One Toast Lightning
Bolts with Coddled Egg .... **GF*, V**

Soups & Starters

Slug Club Christmas Party Spiced Nuts .... **GF, V**
Bubbling Cauldron Bites .... **GF, V**
Swedish Short-Snout's Steak Tartare .... **GF***
Yule Ball Cocktail Shrimp .... **GF**
Slughorn's Appetizer Roll-Ups .... **GF, V*, V+***
Nicolas Flamel Vichyssoise Soup .... **GF, V**
Hagrid's One-Pot Pumpkin Stew .... **GF, V, V+**
Leaky Cauldron's Roasted Tomato Soup with
Marmite Grilled Cheese .... **GF*, V, V+***

Breads & Sides

The Burrow Welcome Wreath .... **V**
Sprout's Superior Sprouts .... **GF**
Grimmauld Place Dinner Rolls .... **V**
Sirius Black Hearth Potatoes .... **GF, V, V+***
Weasley Sweater Focaccia .... **V, V+**
Hogwarts Yorkshire Pudding .... **V***

Mains

Greenhouse Greens Salad .... **GF, V, V+***
Madam Pomfrey's Hospitality Shepherd's Pie .... **GF, V**
Famous Fire Eaters Spicy Beef Skewers .... **GF**
Marauder's Map Tart
Golden Egg Meat Pies
Christmas Eve Beef Roast .... **GF**
Christmas Day Rack of Lamb .... **GF**
Grimmauld Place Roast Turkey Feast .... **GF***
Beauxbatons French Fish .... **GF**
Yule Ball English Fish Pie .... **GF**

Desserts

Golden Snitch Popcorn Balls .... **GF, V***
Hagrid's Pumpkin Seed Brittle .... **GF, V**
Every Flavor Cake Pops .... **V**
Mini Mincemeat Tarts .... **V**
Great Hall Holiday Fruitcake .... **V**
Harry's Favorite Treacle Tart .... **V**
Snowy Burrow Cake .... **V**
Sleepy Cupcakes .... **V**
Great Hall Floating Candle Cake .... **V**
Wizard Chess Pie .... **V**
Butterscotch Ice Cream Pie .... **GF*, V**
"I'm Sorry, Neville" Biscuit Pops .... **V**
Common Room Jam Sandwich Biscuits .... **V**
Shortbread Christmas Biscuits .... **V**
Golden Trio Biscuits .... **V**
Professor Trelawney's Pots de Créme .... **GF, V**
Hogsmeade Invisible Snowballs .... **V**
Flitwick's Christmas Figgy Pudding .... **V**
Butterscotch Ice Cream .... **GF, V**
Triwizard Trifle .... **V**

Drinks

Hot Chocolate Brooms .... **GF*, V**
Hogwarts Punch .... **GF, V, V+***
Durmstrang Punch .... **GF, V, V+**
Beauxbatons Punch .... **GF, V, V+**
Cast a Christmas Spell Spiced Cider .... **GF, V, V+**
Professor Trelawney's
Fortified Earl Grey Tea .... **GF, V, V+**
Hair of the Cat .... **GF, V, V+**
Magical Mulled Wine .... **GF, V, V+***
Mistletoe Cocktail .... **GF, V, V+**
Pumpkin Fizz .... **V**
Black Lake Simple Syrup .... **GF, V, V+**
Black and Orange .... **GF, V, V+**
The Grey Lady .... **GF**

INSIGHT
EDITIONS

PO Box 3088—San Rafael, CA 94912
www.insighteditions.com

𝔣 Find us on Facebook: www.facebook.com/InsightEditions
🄳 Follow us on Twitter: @insighteditions
🄾 Follow us on Instagram: @insighteditions

ISBN: 979-8-88663-088-6
B&N Exclusive ISBN: 979-8-88663-496-9
Gift ISBN: 979-8-88663-298-9

Publisher: Raoul Goff
VP, Co-Publisher: Vanessa Lopez
VP, Creative: Chrissy Kwasnik
VP, Manufacturing: Alix Nicholaeff
VP, Group Managing Editor: Vicki Jaeger
Publishing Director: Jamie Thompson
Senior Designer: Judy Wiatrek Trum
Editor: Anna Wostenberg
Editorial Assistant: Sami Alvarado
Managing Editor: Maria Spano
Senior Production Editor: Michael Hylton
Production Associate: Deena Hashem
Senior Production Manager,
Subsidiary Rights: Lina s Palma-Temena

Photographer: Ted Thomas
Prop and Food Stylist: Elena P. Craig
Assistant Food Stylist: Lauren Tedeschi
Assistant Food Stylist: Patricia Parrish
Photography Art Direction: Judy Wiatrek Trum
Interior Design: Mikaela Buck
Illustrations: Paula Hanback

Insight Editions, in association with Roots of Peace, will plant two trees for each tree used in the manufacturing of this book.
Roots of Peace is an internationally renowned humanitarian organization dedicated to eradicating land mines worldwide and
converting war-torn lands into productive farms and wildlife habitats. Roots of Peace will plant two million fruit and nut trees in
Afghanistan and provide farmers there with the skills and support necessary for sustainable land use.

Manufactured in China by Insight Editions
10 9 8 7 6 5 4 3 2 1